CHURCHES OF SUSSEX

JOHN E. VIGAR

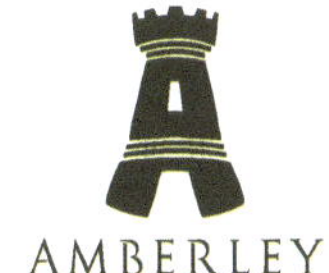

AMBERLEY

This edition first published 2024

Amberley Publishing
The Hill, Stroud
Gloucestershire GL5 4EP

www.amberley-books.com

British Library Cataloguing in Publication Data.
A catalogue record for this book is available from the British Library.

ISBN 978 1 3981 1861 4 (print)
ISBN 978 1 3981 1862 1 (ebook)

Typesetting by SJmagic DESIGN SERVICES, India.
Printed in Great Britain.

Appointed GPSR EU Representative: Easy Access System Europe Oü, 16879218
Address: Mustamäe tee 50, 10621, Tallinn, Estonia
Contact Details: gpsr.requests@easproject.com, +358 40 500 3575

CONTENTS

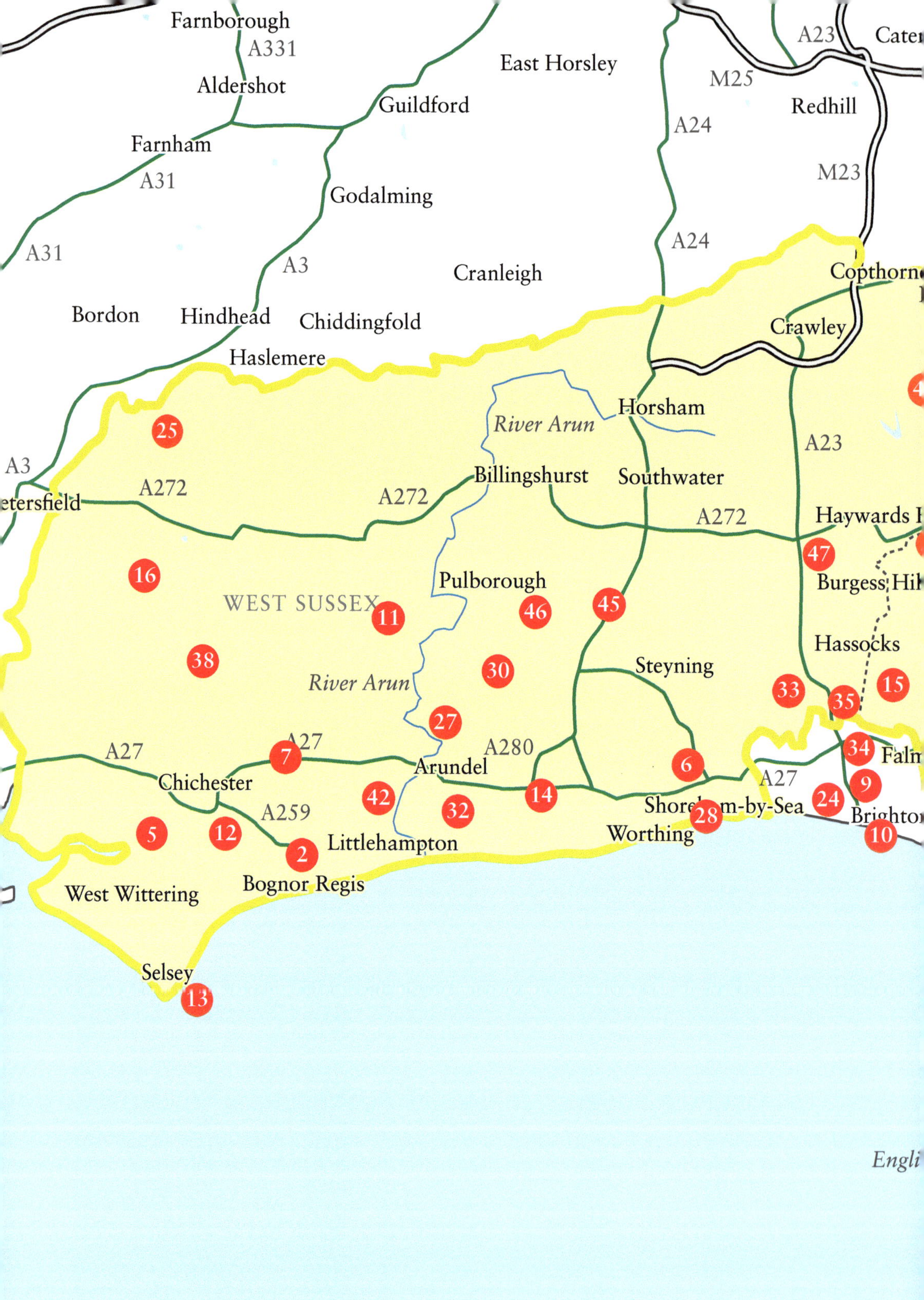

Farnborough
A331
Aldershot
Farnham
A31
A31
Bordon
Hindhead
Haslemere
Guildford
East Horsley
Godalming
A3
Cranleigh
Chiddingfold
etersfield
A272
25
A272
16
WEST SUSSEX
38
River Arun
11
River Arun
A27
7
A27
Chichester
A259
5
12
2
West Wittering
Bognor Regis
Littlehampton
Selsey
13
River Arun
Horsham
Billingshurst
Southwater
A272
Pulborough
46
45
30
27
Arundel
A280
42
32
14
M25
A24
A24
M23
A23
Redhill
Copthorne
Crawley
Cater
A23
Haywards H
47
Burgess Hil
Hassocks
Steyning
33
35
15
6
34
Fal
A27
Shoreham-by-Sea
Worthing
28
24
9
Brighton
10
Engli

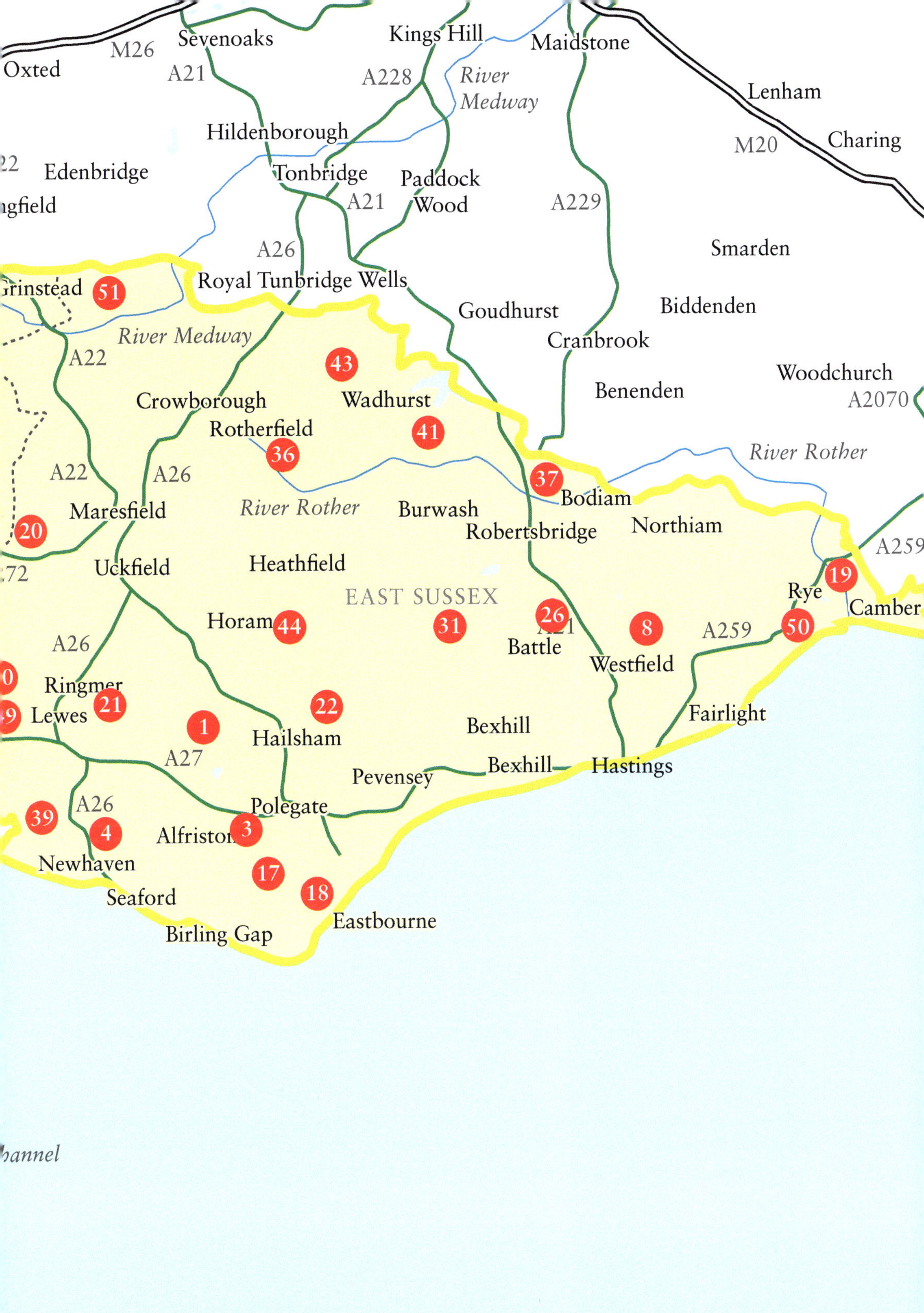

Oxted
M26
Sevenoaks
A21
Kings Hill
A228
Maidstone
River Medway
Lenham
M20
Charing
Edenbridge
ngfield
Hildenborough
Tonbridge
A21
Paddock Wood
A229
Smarden
A26
Royal Tunbridge Wells
Goudhurst
Biddenden
Cranbrook
Woodchurch
A2070
Grinstead
51
River Medway
A22
43
Crowborough
Wadhurst
Benenden
A22
Rotherfield
41
River Rother
A26
36
37
Bodiam
Northiam
River Rother
A259
Maresfield
River Rother
Burwash
Robertsbridge
20
Uckfield
Heathfield
EAST SUSSEX
Rye
19
72
Camber
A26
Horam
44
31
26
8
A259
50
0
Ringmer
Battle
Westfield
9
Lewes
21
22
Fairlight
1
Bexhill
Hailsham
A27
Bexhill
Hastings
Pevensey
A26
39
4
Polegate
3
Alfriston
Newhaven
17
Seaford
18
Birling Gap
Eastbourne
hannel
5km
N

INTRODUCTION

Sussex is a huge county, the parish churches of which deserve to be better known. The local geology has given us buildings of local sandstone and flint, but we also see imported stone from the continent. Monastic communities influenced even the smallest of churches in both their structure and decoration and its early industries of wool production and later iron smelting provided funds that were directed to the improvement of its places of worship. The best-known parish churches from a visitor's point of view are probably Rye and Arundel but in a book which can only cover 10 per cent of Anglican churches in Sussex I wanted to draw attention to the little-known gems which, together, give an overview of period, building materials and social history, and which I think are especially worthwhile. In a period of declining congregations, it is donations from visitors that can make a real difference to keeping churches going and the benefit of tourism has long been recognised in the county. The majority of Sussex churches are open every day or have arrangements for the key to be collected. Some even have help-yourself refreshment tables for visitors. Most churches display historical information, or sell guidebooks to assist the visitor, but the comprehensive website www.sussexparishchurches.org, run by John Allen, contains a detailed history of each and can be wholeheartedly recommended. In my work with churches countrywide I return to Sussex time and again for its exceptional breadth of architecture, variety of landscape, invention and reinvention, and more than anything else for the unique atmosphere of its parish churches, the majority of which have been loved for over thirty generations.

1. ARLINGTON, ST PANCRAS

Set in a textbook country churchyard, this Saxon building has a surprise. It contains the largest collection of thirteenth-century stone coffin lids to be found in a Sussex parish church. You had to be someone of importance to be buried in church, and it was usually in a coffin cut from a single block of stone and set into the ground just deep enough for the cover to be dropped on top to sit flush with the floor. Here, more than half a dozen testify to an important medieval community. Some of these lids are carved with different designs of cross, whilst others are plain. In the thirteenth century people were usually buried right against the wall so the grave wouldn't be in the way. Today the covers stand upright, so there is no knowing exactly where they were, and more importantly no way of telling who once occupied them! By the fourteenth century special alcoves or recesses were constructed over graves and in the north wall of the chancel is a superb example. The coffin it was built for is still in situ, so its cover is better preserved than the others in the church. The chancel and nave are divided by a rood screen which dates from the nineteenth century, but the ensemble gives a good impression of how most churches might have looked before the Reformation when screens were declared illegal. Traces of wall paintings throughout the church present a difficult to decipher palimpsest of designs dating over a period of 500 years. The general rule is that if you can read the text in English it is post-Reformation. The give-away Saxon feature at Arlington is the double-splayed window in the south wall of the nave which was designed before windows had the benefit of glass, so the open part of the window was recessed into the wall to stop leaves and sticks blowing in. In the chancel south wall is a low side window. We now believe that these windows which originally had shutters (one of the hinges remains in the inside) were thrown open at the Consecration, the holiest part of Mass, to create a breeze that made the candles and lamps on top of the rood screen flicker – a bit of 'holy theatre' if you like. Until recently some people called them 'lepers windows' but we now understand that lepers were not allowed freedom in the medieval world and lived in separate communities. But the one thing every visitor will remember of their excursion to this church will be the earthenware vessel behind glass in the north chapel. This a rare acoustic jar, originally built into the wall of the building, on its side with the mouth opening into the church. As a set of possibly four or five they would have greatly improved the volume for those elsewhere in the building. At Etchingham in the east of the county they were set under the stalls. Before leaving Arlington look at the embroidery on the Lady Chapel altar and discover the birds, mammals and roses which are a delight.

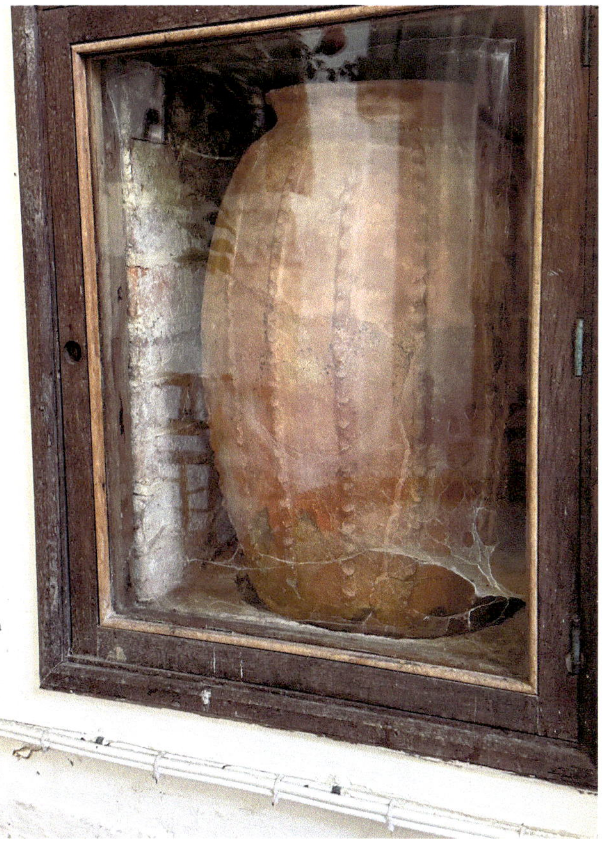

Arlington. This rare acoustic jar would have been built into the church wall during the medieval period, with its mouth exposed to help amplify the services.

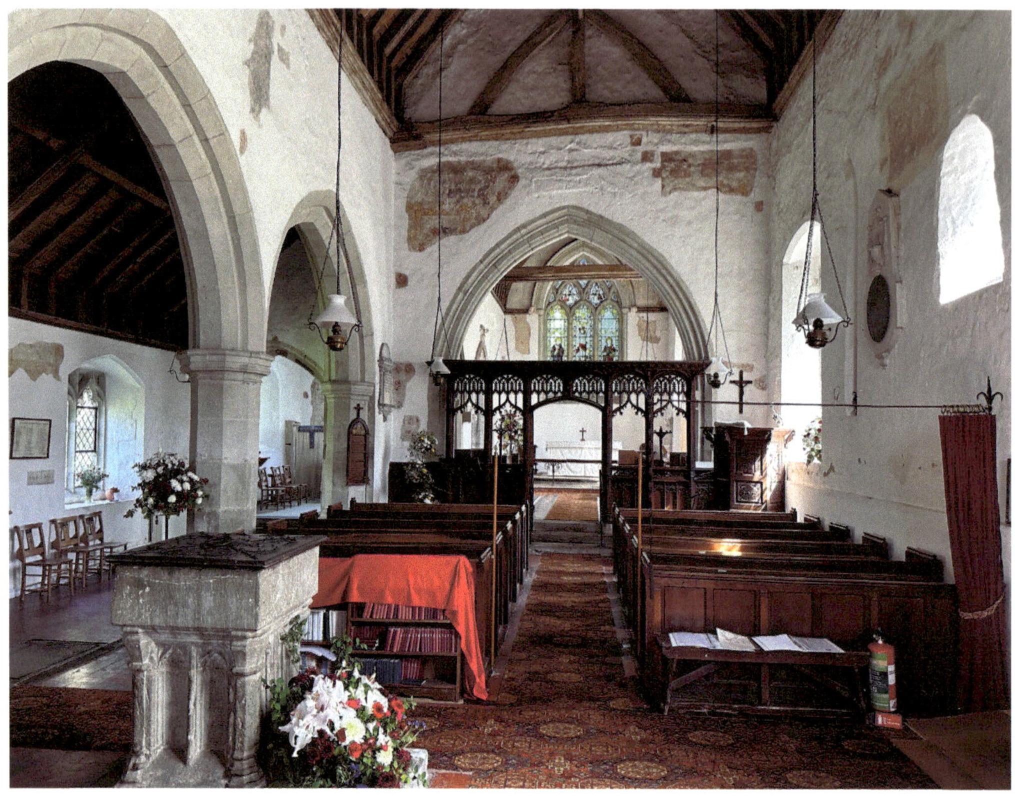

Arlington. In this view we see the remains of several layers of medieval wall painting, the fourteenth-century arcade to the north aisle and the nineteenth-century rood screen.

2. BARNHAM, ST MARY

In an area full of sumptuous thirteenth-century churches, it is refreshing to find one at the humble end of the scale, in this instance standing far from its village centre. St Mary's is a Norman building, remodelled firstly in the thirteenth century and again in the fifteenth after which it found itself stuck in a pleasant time warp, not suffering alterations each time new money came into the village. As a result, this much-loved and well-cared for church is appreciated not only by its congregation but by its many visitors. As you walk up the path you can see the character of the church by its lancet windows which, on the outside, have no mouldings around the tops to deflect rainwater. Even the slightly later two-light windows have no hood moulds, making the glass they contained susceptible to damage by rainwater carrying grit down. Where money was no object hood moulds were essential. When you step into the interior you realise how simple this building is, with no structural distinction between nave and chancel. The walls, however, show that there was once a north aisle, added at a time when money was plentiful in the thirteenth century and removed around a hundred years later when they could no longer afford to maintain it. The late Norman font is much weathered so must have been thrown outside at some stage. The three stained-glass lancets in the east window date from 1947 and were designed by Joan Fulleylove, an artist in the Arts and Crafts period who also produced artwork for the Suffrage movement. Easily missed is a short graffiti inscription by the organ, now protected behind glass. Although it is not credited to an individual, it reads 'Pray for the soul of my father who died at Agincourt' and is a rare local record of an international event.

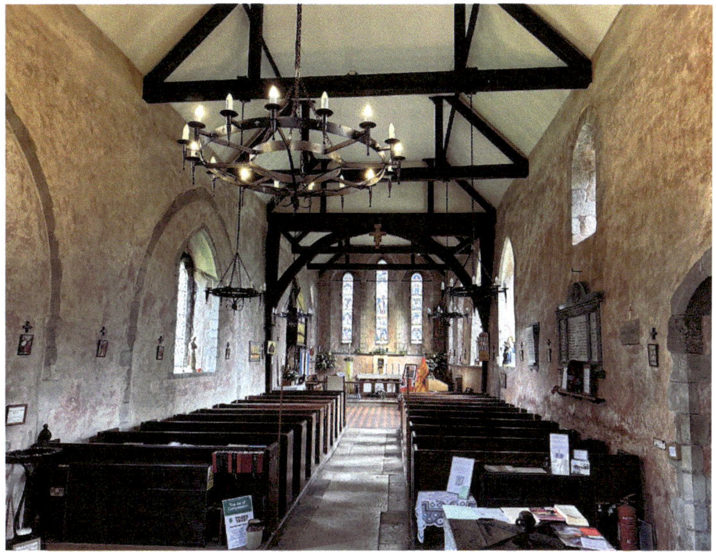

Barnham. On the left are the blocked arches to the former north aisle. The small window on the right is Norman, whilst the division between nave and chancel is formed by a wooden brace supporting the tie beam.

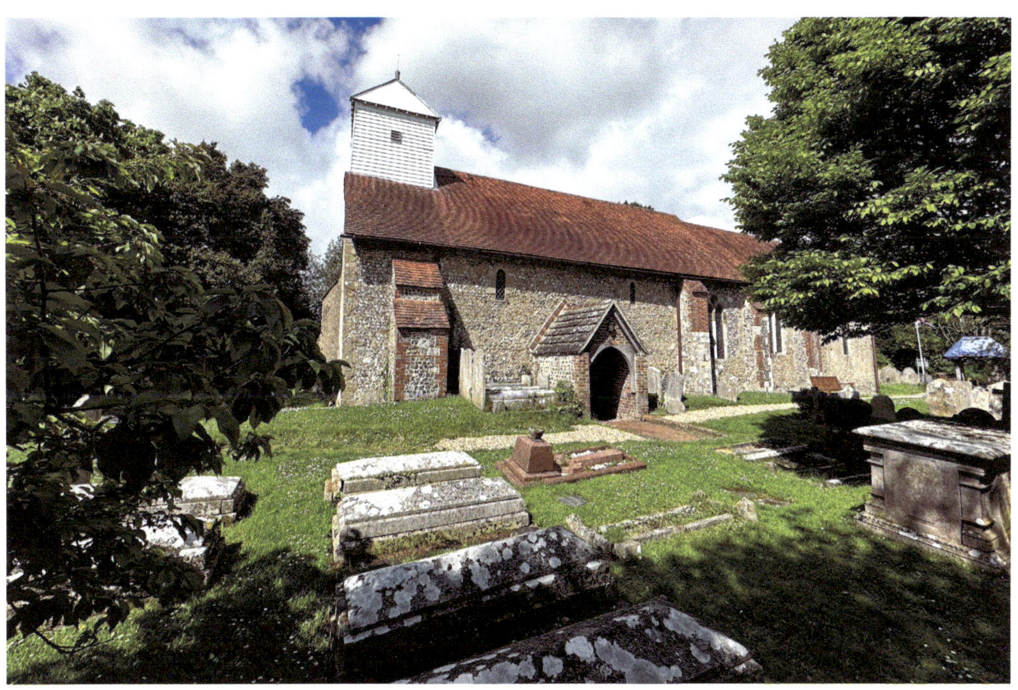

Barnham. The south wall shows two original Norman windows, coursed flint walling, Horsham slab roof on the porch and weatherboarded bellcote.

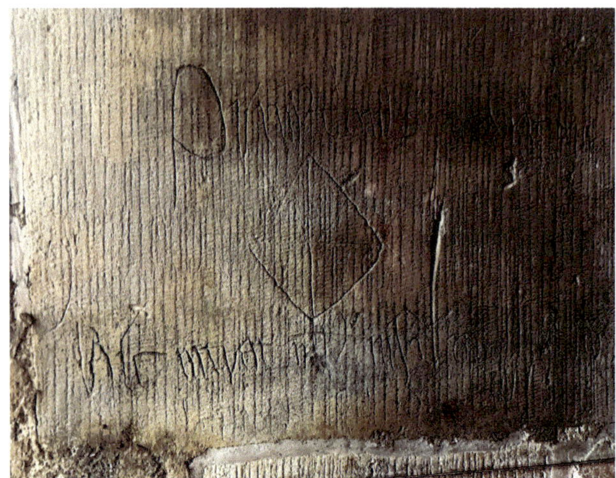

Left: Barnham. This scratched Latin inscription by the organ asks for prayers for a man who died at the Battle of Agincourt in 1415.

Below: Barnham. A detail of the east window of 1949 by Joan Fulleylove depicting angelic cherubs.

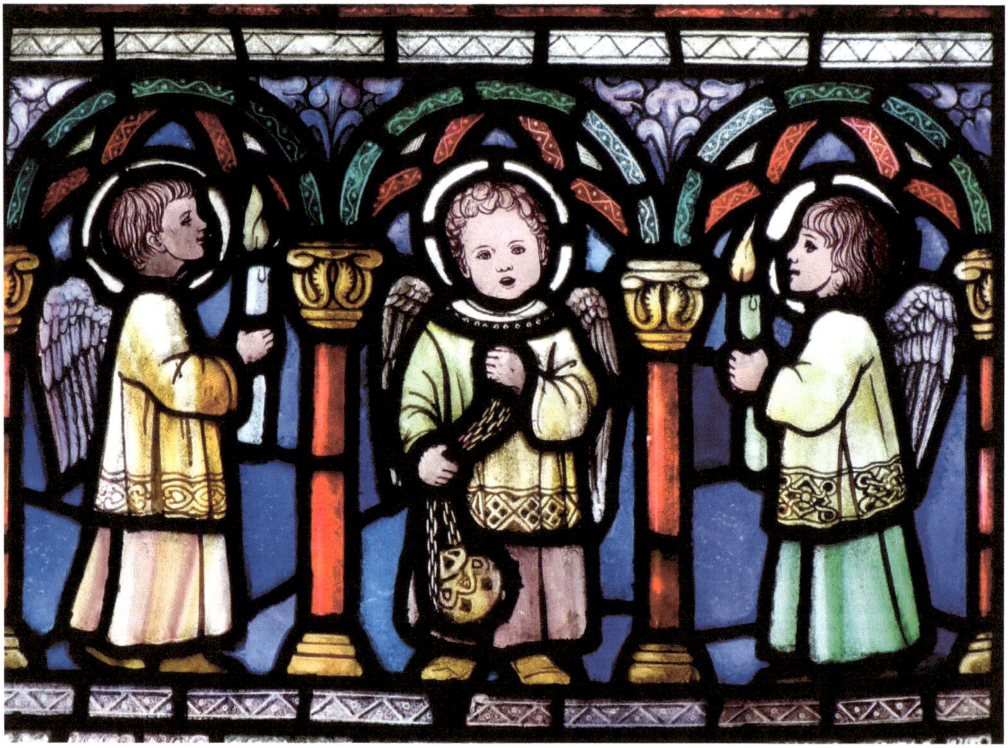

3. Berwick, St Michael and All Angels

Nobody today would believe that in 1941 the introduction of the decorative scheme which has made this church famous was the subject of much controversy. It had stemmed from the loss of much stained glass due to bomb damage and the idea was to provide colour through applied decoration and to replace the stained-glass windows with clear glass. The fact that the main artists, Duncan Grant and Vanessa Bell, lived locally gave the parish a unique opportunity, but still there was opposition. Eventually a Consistory Court was held and permission granted. Eighty years later visitors come from across the globe to revel in the amazing interior paintings, and the visitor is unlikely ever to be alone. There is a switch for visitor lighting and the church has recently undergone a much-appreciated reordering. Most of the art people come to see are not true murals, as they were painted on boards that were then affixed to the walls. The four large paintings depict the Annunciation, Nativity, Christ in Glory, and the Victory of Calvary. In the Nativity scene there is lots of local flavour with recognisable landscapes and characters, whilst the painting over the chancel arch includes the then Rector and Bishop. Other paintings in the church were executed by Bell's son and daughter, whilst the altar frontal of Our Lady and Child was made by Duncan Grant's mother. Don't miss the Wise and Foolish Virgins high in the chancel, or the delightful paintings on the chancel side of the screen. Recently the scheme has been enhanced by a painted reredos of a local country lane with wildflowers and a rainbow. For those less enamoured of the modern art there is an early plain tub font, an outsize Easter Sepulchre and a much-remodelled fourteenth-century sedilia.

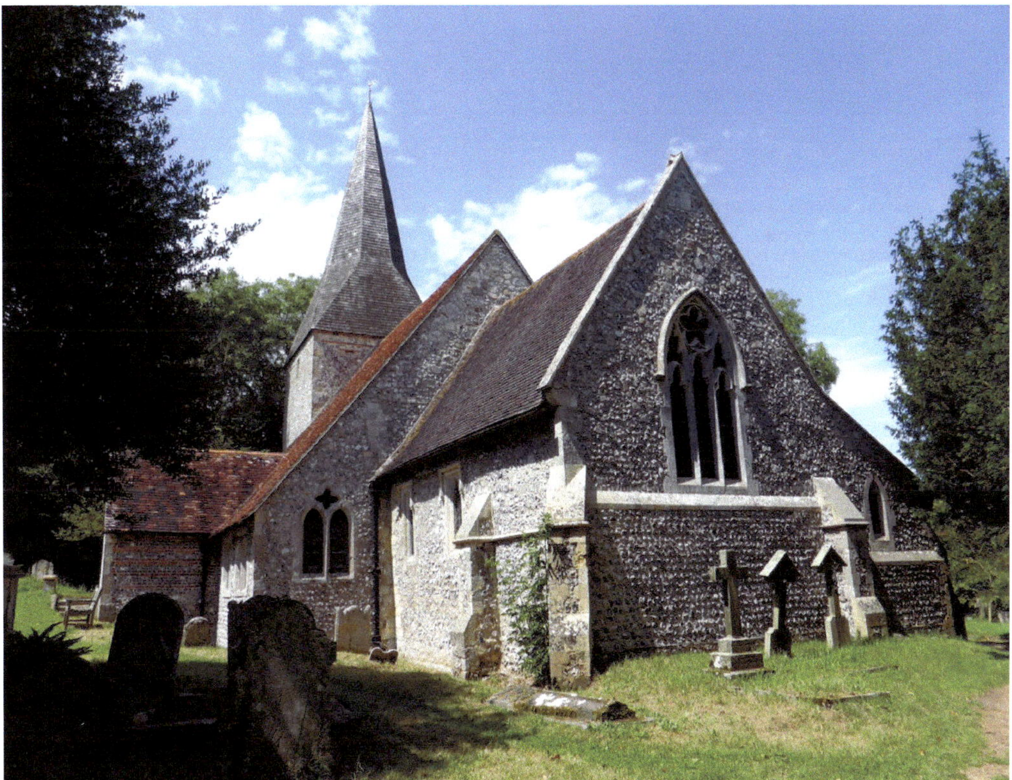

Berwick. This exterior view from the east shows a catslide roof which covers the nave and south aisle in one sweep. (Image by Paul Farmer)

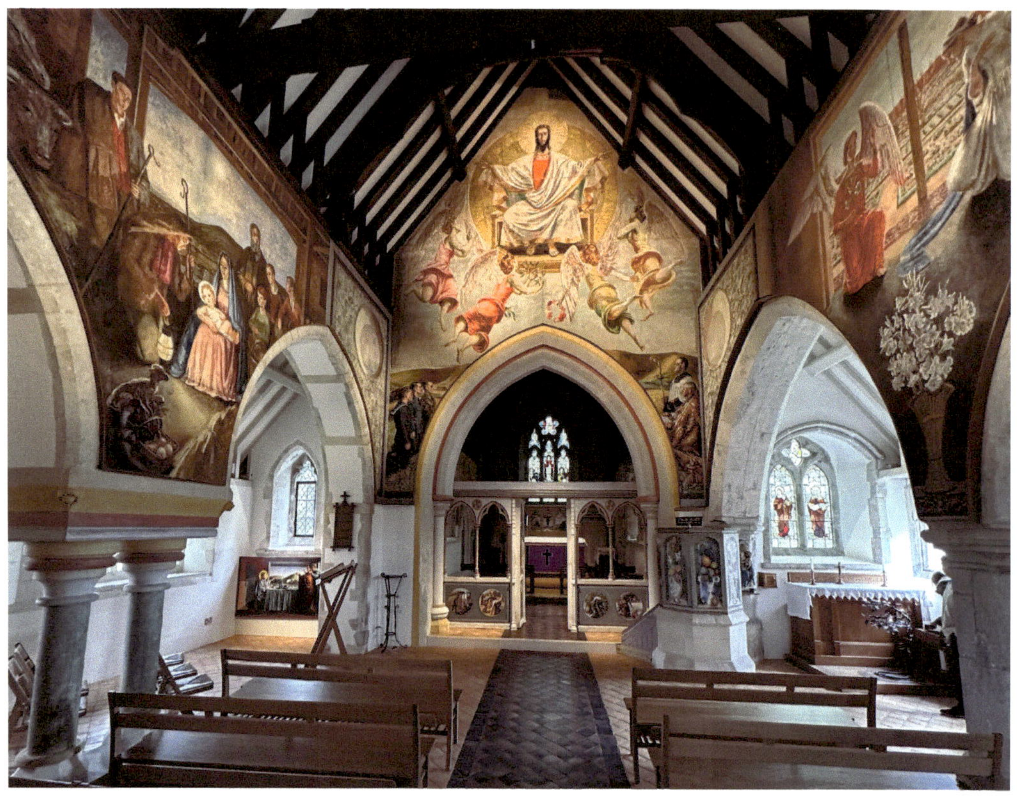

Berwick. The rich interior, primarily by Duncan Grant and Vanessa Bell, includes allusions to local topography and includes portraits of local residents. The nativity scene on the left shows a Sussex trug and crooks.

4. BISHOPSTONE, ST ANDREW

This picturesque church, standing in an isolated location just over a mile from the sea, gives us some of the best Saxon work in the county. To me, the situation of the site is more than anything a clue to its antiquity. Protected from the coast yet close enough to facilitate travel, this may be one of the earliest church sites in the county. The walls are of flint and quite thin, typically Saxon, and exhibit several Saxon features including long and short work at the quoins. However, the most important visible part of the structure is the south porticus. This was a tall burial chapel, originally only accessible from inside the church like the example still to be seen at Breamore in Hampshire. Here at Bishopstone the Normans converted it to a porch when they built their tower which then blocked the original west door. Their Romanesque arch is clear to see in the porticus and above it, in the original wall, is a Saxon sundial with the name Eadric inscribed on it. Was this the name of the person buried in the porticus? The fact that the name is accompanied by a cross, as in a bishop's signature, suggests so and also ties in nicely with the place name. However, there is no recorded Eadric as a Saxon bishop of Chichester, so he may have been an assistant, or suffragan, bishop. Internally there is a surprise as the church has a north aisle and is divided internally into three sections, rather than just nave and chancel. Here the detailing is all thirteenth and fourteenth centuries. Just one early survivor is a stone coffin lid now mounted on the wall with three carved roundels, probably early Norman in date. In the chancel is a Georgian memorial tablet to the Revd James Hurdis, Professor of Poetry at Oxford University. The inscription is by his friend and fellow Sussex poet William Hayley.

5. BOSHAM, HOLY TRINITY

It was here that St Wilfred discovered a religious community of Celtic Christians when he arrived as a missionary in the seventh century. Nothing of that date survives today but a substantial church was built in the mid-eleventh century and is famously depicted on the Bayeux Tapestry. Part of the chancel and tower are of that early period, but the nave that joined them together was a simple tall rectangular box without aisles. The latter were added in the thirteenth and fourteenth centuries with simple arcades in the Early English style, the bases of which seem very high until you learn that the floor level was lowered by the Victorians. At the base of the northeast pier are some interesting carved heads. The odd upper area at the east end of the south aisle was built as a chantry chapel above a stone vaulted bone hole, now converted

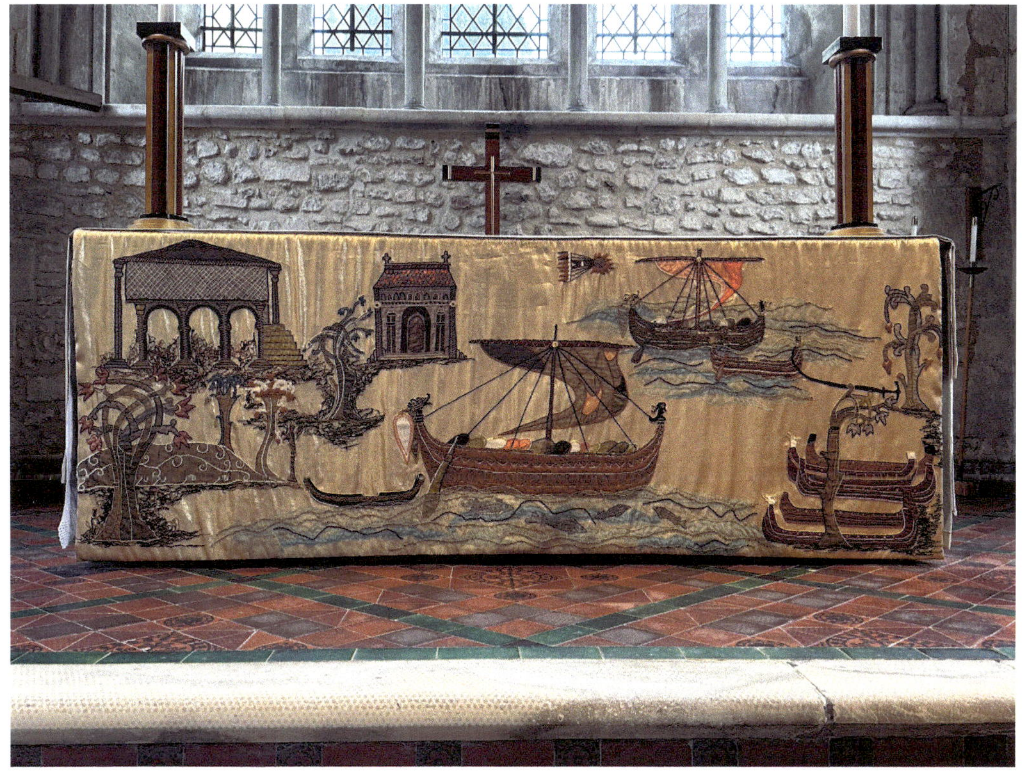

Bosham. The Festival Frontal is inspired by the Bayeux Tapestry and contains an image of Bosham Church as it was depicted there in the eleventh century.

to a chapel, where there are four pieces of late medieval glass imported from the Low Countries. The church contains two tomb recesses. That by the south door has lovely heads carved on each of its four hanging cusps, whilst the superior recess by the organ, of roughly the same fourteenth-century date, now has an effigy inserted into it. What a sight this recess would have been in its original painted form. Opposite this is a very early hutch chest dating from the thirteenth century, simply constructed of planks of wood. The choir stalls have two carved bench ends, one fifteenth century, the other a nineteenth-century copy. Looking back down the church, a triangular window above the Saxon tower arch once led to a west gallery and it is also possible to see the rough join of the rebuilt nave where it meets the earlier tower wall. When first built the interior would have been limewashed, so we are not seeing the church correctly, but in this instance the archaeological interest of the masonry somehow makes it alright. If you're lucky and visit during a church Festival you'll see the altar frontal, the design of which was inspired by the Bayeux Tapestry.

6. BOTOLPH, ST BOTOLPH'S

Known locally as the Wayfarers' Church, this venerable building sits a stone's throw from the South Downs Way where it crosses the River Adur. The river was once a busy waterway, so it is not surprising that the church is dedicated to St Botolph, patron saint of travellers. It has stood here since Saxon times, the periods of wealth and destitution showing in its fabric. Its thirteenth-century west tower with the typical 'Sussex Cap' roof of Horsham slab really doesn't prepare the visitor for the Saxon work to come. The first evidence we get that this is a church of the tenth or eleventh century can be seen on the south wall of the nave. Just above the large thirteenth-century window can be seen the round head of one of the original windows. Typically, it is very high in what are, already, very tall walls. We enter the church through a rustic eighteenth-century brick porch as you might find on any local farmhouse, which shields a door with a delightful date carving of 1630 and the churchwardens' initials, set within a symbol of the Holy Trinity. It is obvious that this church was once much larger as the north wall of the nave contains the blocked arcade to a thirteenth-century aisle which must have been built at the same time as the tower. It was probably demolished in the seventeenth or eighteenth century as the upkeep of the building became a drain on a small population, the medieval village having disappeared. In 1801 the population of the parish was just thirty-six. At the rear of the church the font is one of those that is almost impossible to date, following no architectural pattern, but it probably dates from the seventeenth century. The chancel arch is Saxon, but not as tall as others in the county, suggesting it is late – about the time of the Norman Conquest. Fragments of wall paintings remain on the east wall of the nave, dating from the thirteenth-century alterations. The magnificent pulpit with a chunky carved canopy is Jacobean. In front of the chancel arch is a stone coffin lid covering the grave of someone of importance – was this the lay person who financed the thirteenth-century enlargements? In the south wall of the chancel is a low-side window. Local tradition associates these windows with lepers but we now believe that these shuttered openings were for better ventilation of the chancel and one of the hinges that supported the shutter survives. The church has several monuments to the Penfold family who later emigrated to Australia to found Penfold Wines.

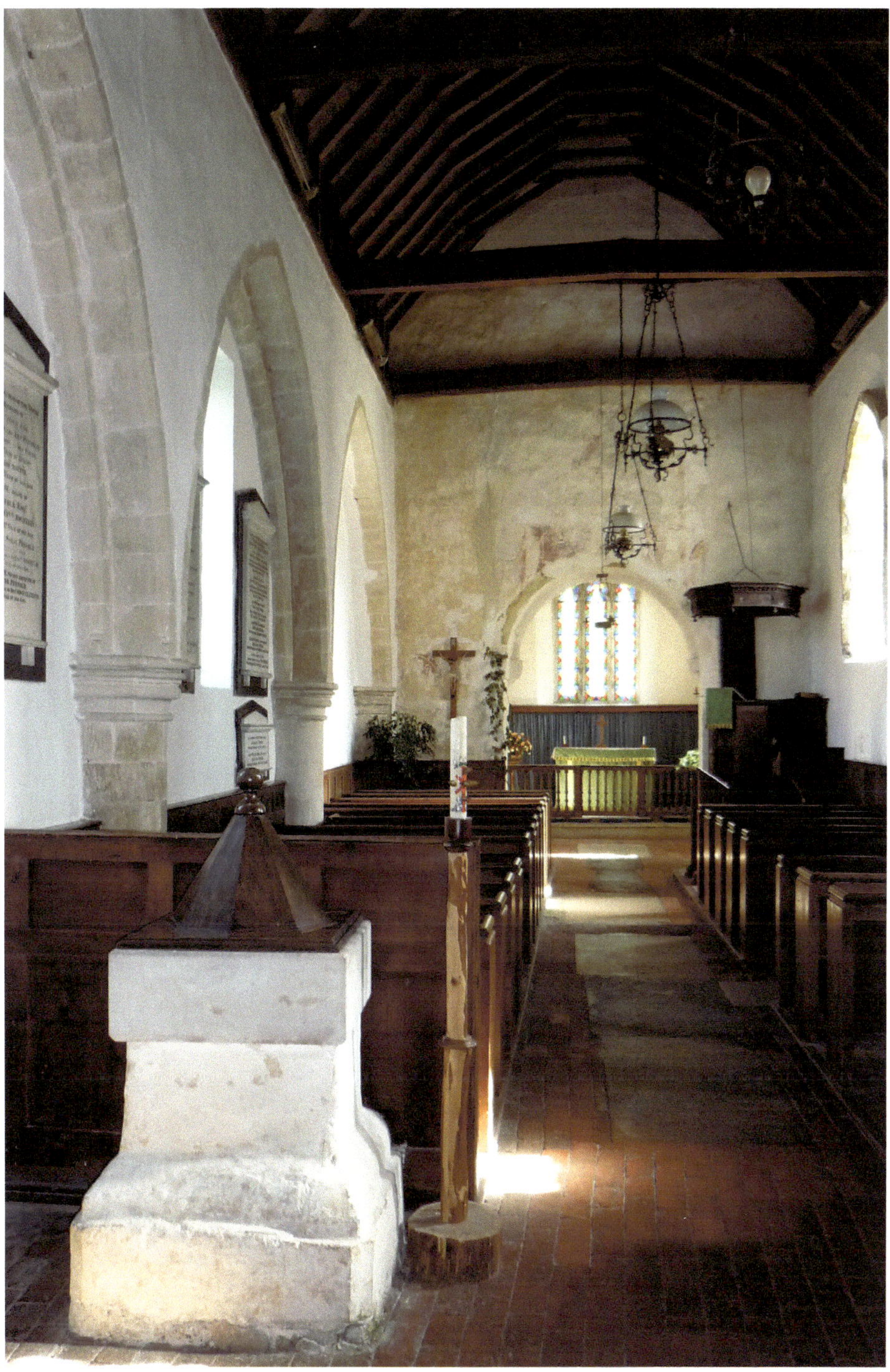

Botolphs. When the thirteenth-century north aisle was taken down the piers and capitals were left intact. This view also shows the chancel arch and the wall tablets of the Penfold family.

7. BOXGROVE, SS MARY AND BLAISE

One of the must-visit Sussex churches, this comprises the eastern end of a monastic church that lost its nave at the Dissolution of the Monasteries. If you approach from the west, you'll see from the ruins that the monastic house was to the north of the church. We enter through a porch into the south aisle of the church which would have stretched as far to your left as it now does to your right. As a major cruciform building it has transepts which are confusing to the visitor as they now stand close to the west end of the church. Perhaps it's easier if you look at the west wall where you will find two blocked doorways. This wall was once the stone screen which divided the monastic part where we are standing from the parochial nave to the west. To the south are two round-headed arches from the original Norman building, whilst the rest of the present building is a remodelling of the thirteenth century which gives us some of the grandest architecture of its period in the county. The arcade has octagonal piers at first which give way to circular piers and then composite piers made up of clusters of black Purbeck marble. This speaks of wealth. Many visitors comment on the painted ceiling. This was the work of Lambert Barnard in the early sixteenth century when he was employed by Earl de la Warre to portray his family heraldry. De la Warre was also responsible for the outstanding chantry chapel to

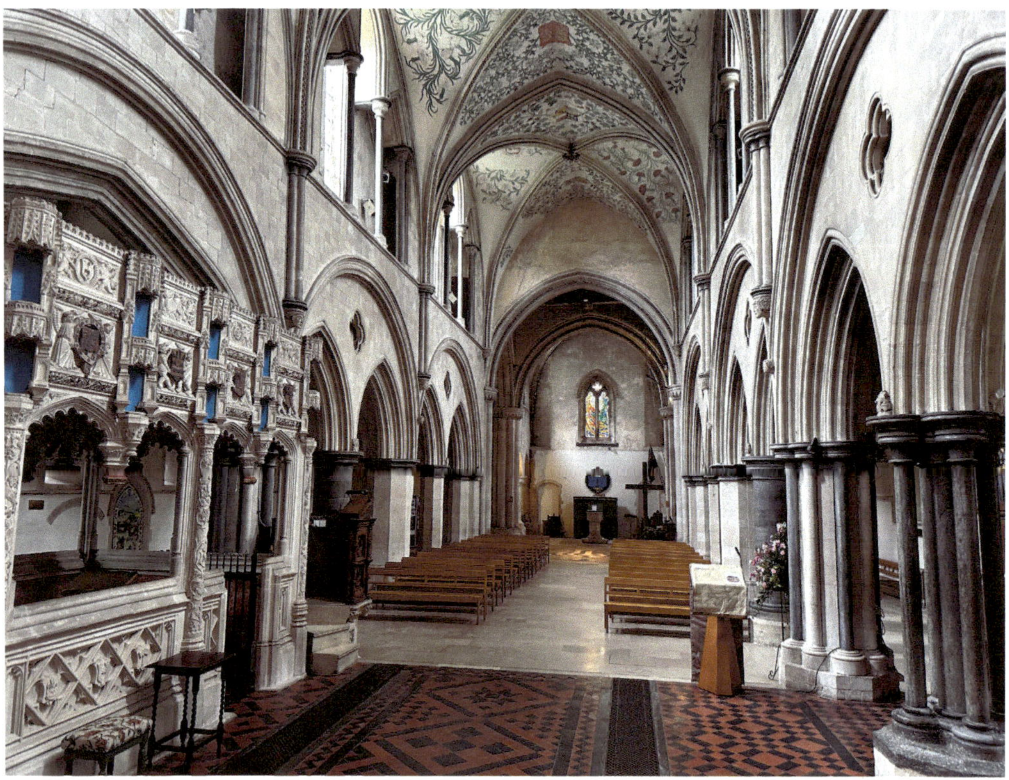

Boxgrove. Looking west. On the left is the De la Warre chantry chapel. The architecture of the interior is thirteenth century with the use of Purbeck marble on the piers and the ceiling painting is by Lambert Barnard and dates from the sixteenth century.

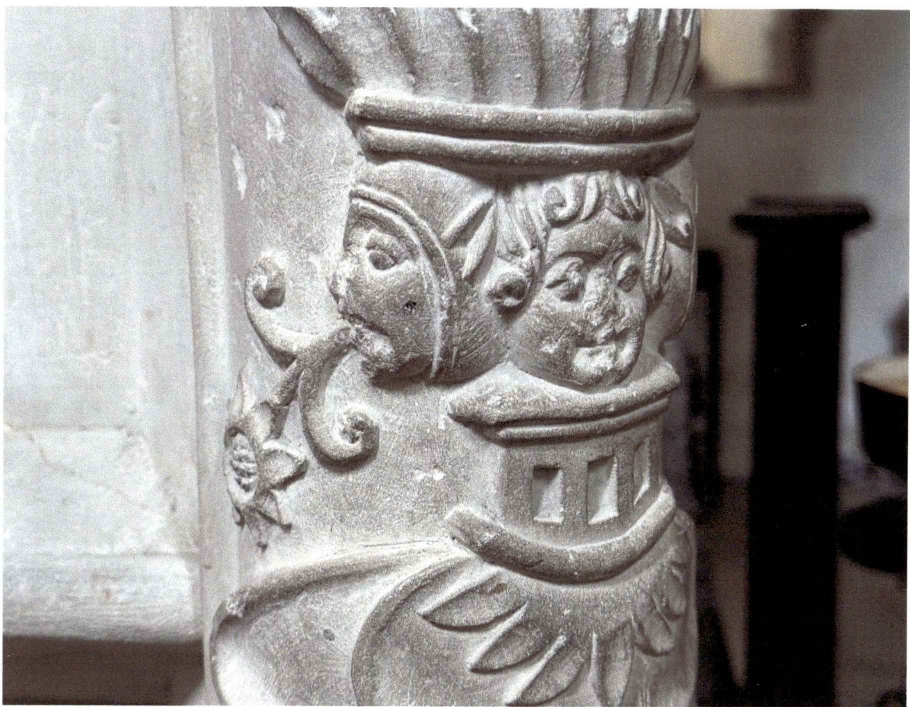

Boxgrove. The delicate carving on the sixteenth-century De la Warre chantry includes this foliage spewer, a subvariant of the more familiar foliate head.

the south of the altar. It is one of the most important in England and rather better than many in our cathedrals. In essence it is a completely free-standing chapel built to house an altar for masses to be said for Lord de la Warre's soul. Dating from 1532, it is a charming mixture of Gothic and classical forms. Internally the chantry is famed for the pendants terminating in Tudor roses descending from the vault, but it is the outside where the visitor can spend hours searching for tiny details. My favourite is the scene depicting the well-dressed prince who comes across a living skeleton and is obviously being told 'As I am, so shall you be'. On another corner we find Daniel wrestling a lion. Elsewhere the stained glass includes a Victorian east window by Michael O'Connor and two late twentieth-century windows. One by Mel Howse remembers an American airman killed in the Battle of Britain whilst Nicola Kantorowicz designed the colourful west window in 1998.

8. BREDE, ST GEORGE

A memorable church with wide-ranging views to the south. The oldest part of the structure is at the west end of the nave where circular piers survive from the thirteenth century. A hundred years later the original chancel was demolished and the church extended east. On the site of the old chancel the large arches to north and south were added, but they could not easily be joined onto the existing lower arcades, so a flat section of wall was left to carry the transition. It works so well that many visitors do not even notice it! The alignment of churches depended on the sunrise to determine east, and when the new chancel was laid out the builders took a different centre line which resulted in the anomaly that the south wall of the chancel is shorter by over 40 cm than the north to give a straight east wall. Much of this work would have been paid for by the Oxenbridge family of Brede Place who eventually built their own chapel at the south-east corner in 1537 to take the monument to Sir Goddard Oxenbridge (d. 1531). He had been Sheriff of Sussex three times and was summoned to greet the Holy Roman Emperor when he landed at Dover in May 1522. His monument is of Caen stone, which, in Sussex, we more usually associate with Norman work, and shows him in armour with a jolly lion at his feet. Confusingly the date shown is of the monument, and not his death. Whilst his two wives do not get effigies with him their ancestry is represented by the coloured heraldic shields at the front of the tomb chest. Linking the chapel with the chancel is an arch into which is carved the complicated heraldry of the Oxenbridge, Hopton, Ore and Etchingham families supported by a male and female Wodewose, a wild person of the woods. A nearby wooden statue of Our Lady and Child is by Clare Sheridan, the sculptor cousin of Sir Winston Churchill, and is a memorial to her son carved from an oak which grew nearby. Another delightful feature, this time near the back of the church, is the Poor Box. The

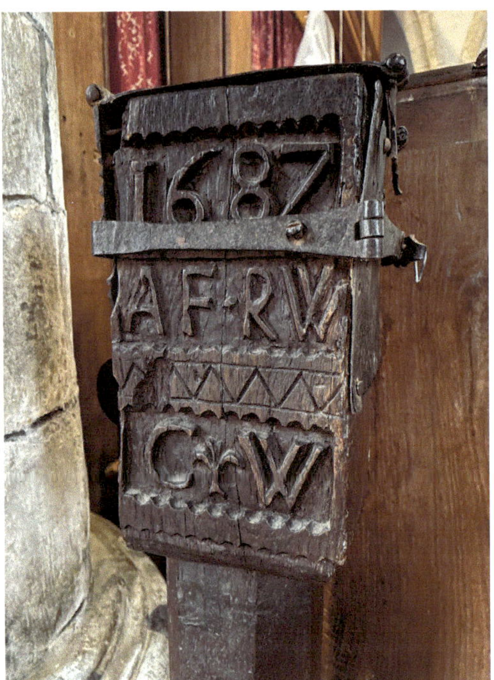

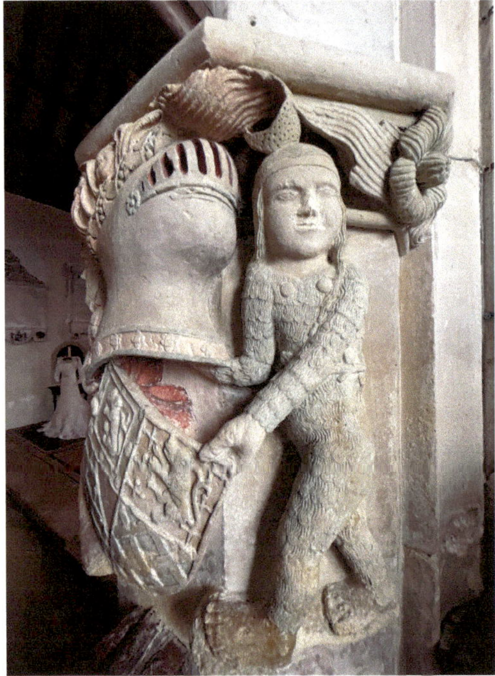

Above left: Brede. The wooden church poor box is dated 1687 and includes the initials of AF and RW who were the two churchwardens (indicated by the CW below). It is made secure by iron fastenings.

Above right: Brede. As a supporter to a shield of arms we find a rare female Wodewose, known as a Fanke. She represents the potential baseness that usually lies dormant in all humans.

iron plate at the top is inscribed 'Sarveth the Lord and remember the Poor', whilst its wooden case gives the date 1687. As you leave the church look high up outside at the junction of the south chapel and the chancel and you will see an inscribed lead panel which records that the gutter was cast by Mr Griffin of Battle in 1665.

9. BRIGHTON, ST BARTHOLOMEW

Seaside towns are the very best places to study Victorian churches. As their populations expanded so church provision was at a premium and new churches were thrown around like confetti. As the quickest-growing early nineteenth-century resort in Britain, Brighton had more than its fair share of new or rebuilt places of worship – over thirty for the Church of England alone. These range in style from the cathedral-like to the simple preaching box, the hidden chapel to the church which completely dominates its landscape. One of the most notable in the latter category is

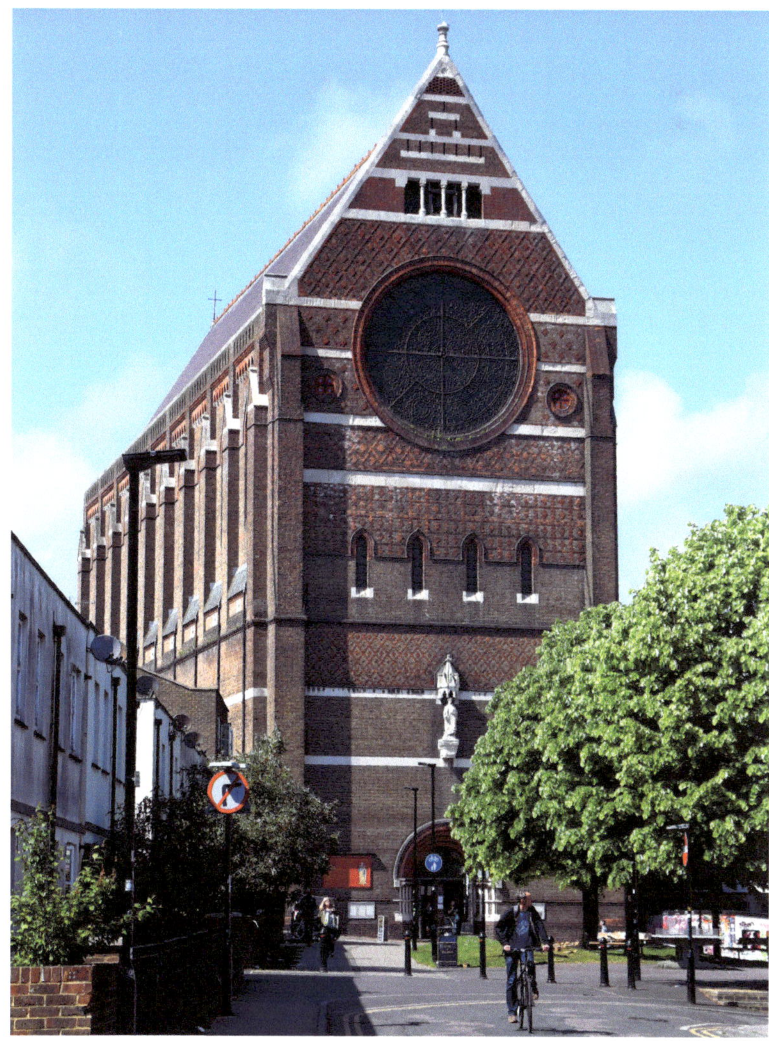

Brighton, St Bartholomew. Dating from 1874, this church towers over the former slum areas north of Brighton station. (Image by Simon Knott)

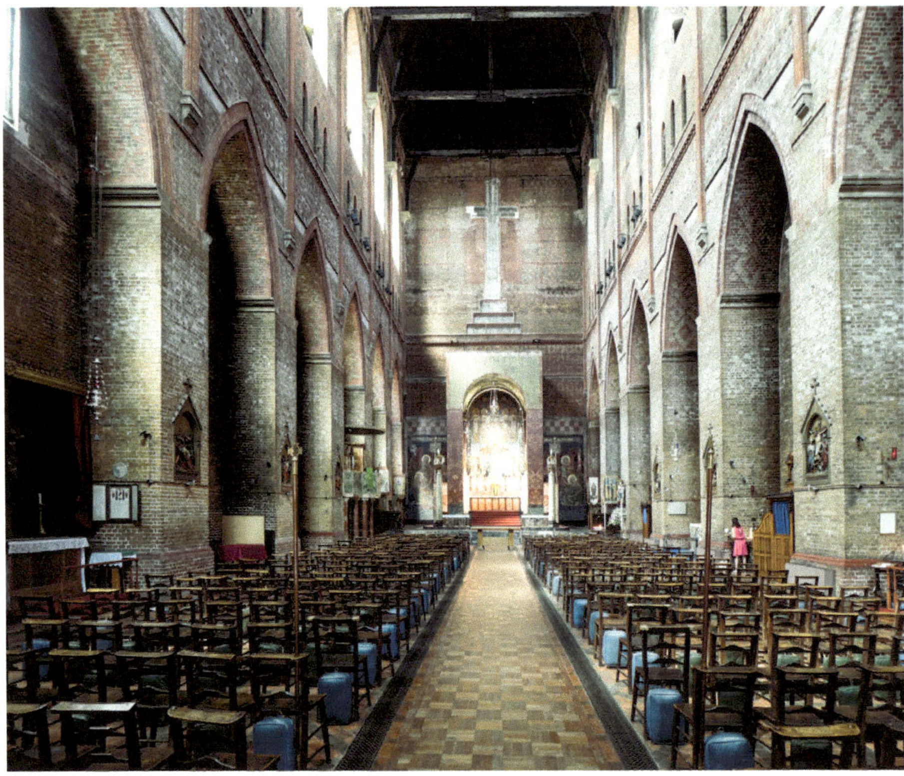

Brighton, St Bartholomew. This is the tallest parish church in England at over 100 feet to the apex of the roof and was designed to bring people to their knees. (Image by John Salmon)

St Bartholomew which towers over the quarter of the town where the road and rail connections arrive from London. Like several Brighton churches it was a product of the munificence of members of the Wagner family, wealthy high church clergymen, and designed to serve the slum houses that had grown up north of the fashionable centre. Building commenced in 1872, designed by a local architect Edmund Scott and built by local builders Stenning and Co., and it still shocks visitors by its scale. Unbelievably it was never completed, so stands as a single brick vessel running parallel to the ridge of land on which it stands. The interior is beautified by appropriate furnishings, mostly added in the decades after the church was opened in 1874. On the east wall is the baldachino or canopy over the High Altar, built of brick and faced with marble. Its designer was the noted Arts and Crafts architect Henry Wilson. Above it a huge cross is picked out in tile and stone where one would normally expect an east window. It is only when we look closely that we realise that the surrounding brick wall isn't plain at all but relieved with polychromatic decoration. The pulpit is also a more recent addition, based on those found in early Italian churches, supported by pillars and faced with green marble. The chairs in the church remind us that there were never benches here and that from the start there were no reserved seats. It was a space for everyone regardless of background that is still much appreciated today.

10. BRIGHTON, ST NICHOLAS

Before Brighton became a fashionable resort it was a fishing town and its residents worshipped at this church on the hill above their closely packed streets. No doubt its tower was used to look out to sea, and its bells rung to help fog-bound ships to return to port. It is dedicated to the patron saint of sailors, St Nicholas, and is mainly fourteenth century in date, although it was substantially restored between 1852 and 1854. This is a rather early date for a restoration compared to most English churches and is explained by the fact that the work commemorated the life of the 1st Duke of Wellington. In fact, there had been plans for years to repair the church but these had come to nothing. Wellingtons' death provided a fresh impetus (he had gone to school

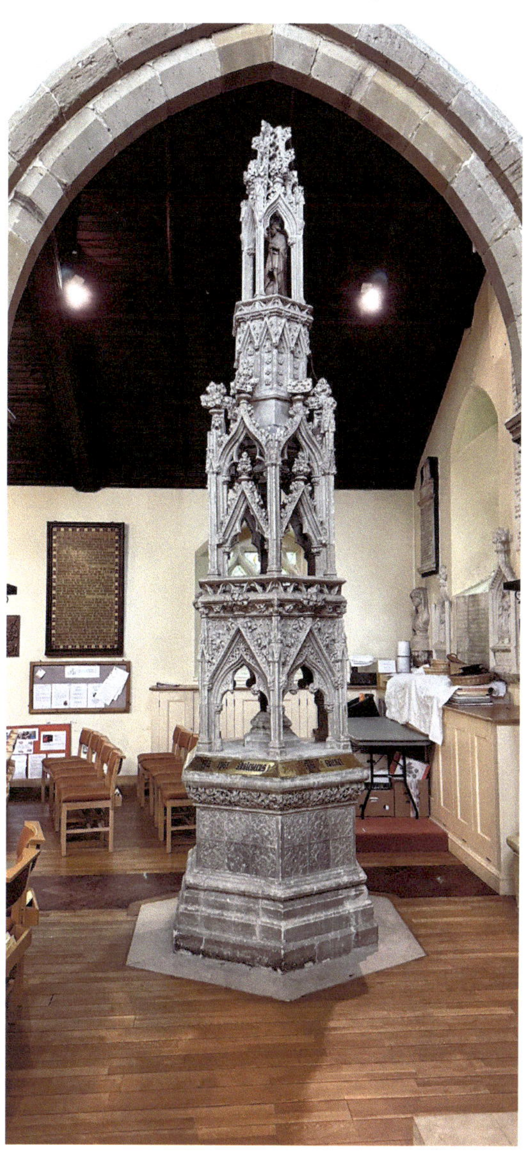

Brighton, St Nicholas. The monument to the 1st Duke of Wellington (d. 1852) dominates the rear of the church with its intricate carving.

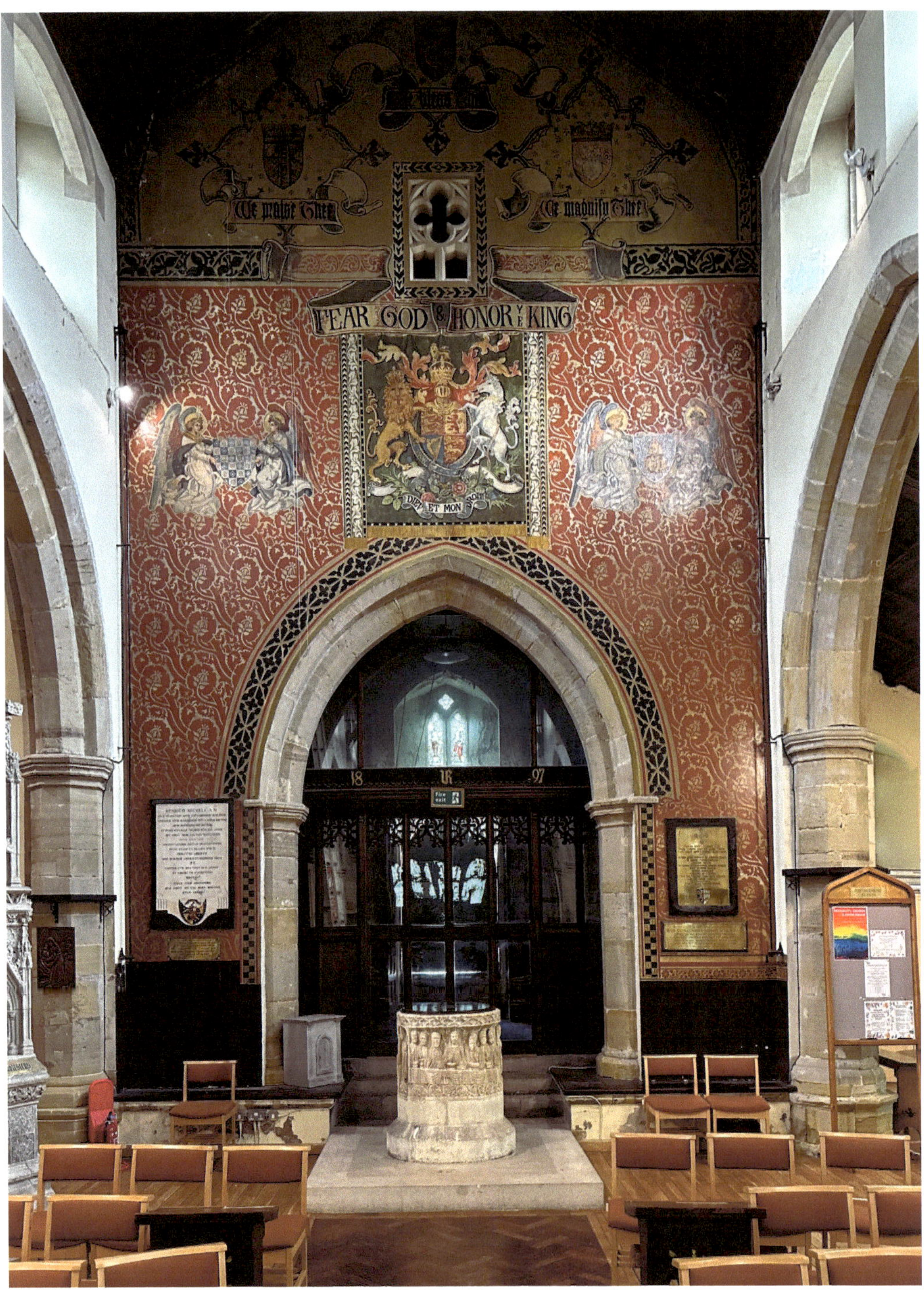

Brighton, St Nicholas. The nineteenth-century stencilled decoration of the church may best be seen on the west wall, where it incorporated an earlier royal arms.

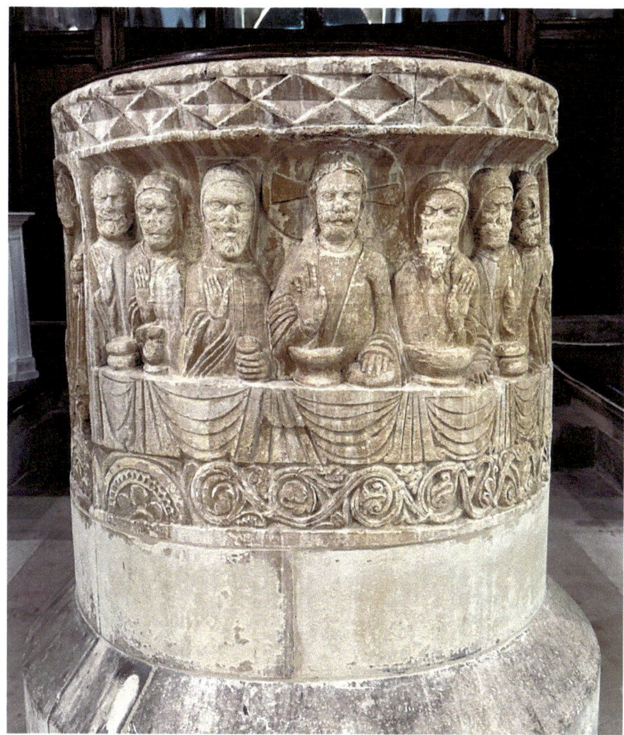

Brighton, St Nicholas. The Romanesque tub font of Caen stone depicts, amongst other scenes, the Last Supper, a rare subject for such an object. It is the oldest furnishing to be found in any Brighton church.

in the Vicarage) and £6,000 was spent, creating the church we see today. Despite this quality work the most spectacular thing to see in the church is the 700-year-old tub font, probably made in France and depicting an odd mixture of scenes, including The Last Supper, the Baptism of Christ and the Life of St Nicholas. I love the stormy sea and the sailing boat made for two in the latter scene. Nearby is a tall memorial to the Duke of Wellington, looking like a lost East Anglian font cover in stone, whilst on the wall is a fantastic glimpse into social history of the time. It is the subscription board listing all those who contributed to the work. The Vicar gave £1,000 followed by the good and the great, those who wished to be seen to have contributed as well as anonymous donations from 'a friend of the Vicar' and corporate gifts from 'The Brighton Gas Light and Coke Company'. It truly is a window into the life of Brighton in 1853. Later in the century the church was further beautified, with work done by local man Charles Eamer Kempe. His is much of the stained glass and the lovely rood on the medieval screen. He also stencilled the walls to the designs of another artist, Somers Clarke, who had studied architecture under Sir Gilbert Scott, and whose father was Parish Clerk here.

11. BURTON, ST RICHARD OF CHICHESTER

This fantastic church punches well above its weight for much is packed into the diminutive building standing adjacent to Burton Park mansion. We have here a two-cell church of ironstone rubble – some of it laid in herringbone form, which suggests an early Norman build. The upper part of the west nave wall has been rebuilt; the quoins of the tower now being formed of brick which are brought down to nearly touch the west window. Entrance is via a west door which brings you into a treasure chest of an interior with important monuments and wall paintings. There is no chancel arch, the division being formed by a fifteenth-century screen where remains of decorative polychrome decoration can just be picked out. Above this the east wall of the nave displays the Decalogue which is painted on plaster. You can also see here that the roof was at some stage plastered as the timbers show the nails that would have supported the laths. In the splay of the north window is a fine painting of an upside-down person with long hair. The jury is still out on their identity, but it may be based on St Uncumber, a Portuguese princess. There are two especially fine memorials in the nave, both table tombs which display brass inscriptions and heraldry. Sir John Goring (1521) has a kneeling figure with four shields of arms but sadly now without an inscription. In any other church this tomb would be a showstopper but here he is upstaged by his son Sir William Goring (1554) whose tomb stands opposite. His stone monument itself is of higher quality and there is far more brass on display, too. Sadly, Sir William has disappeared, as have some of his children, but his wife Elizabeth remains together with several individual inscription plates including two which have been set vertically as there wasn't the space to place

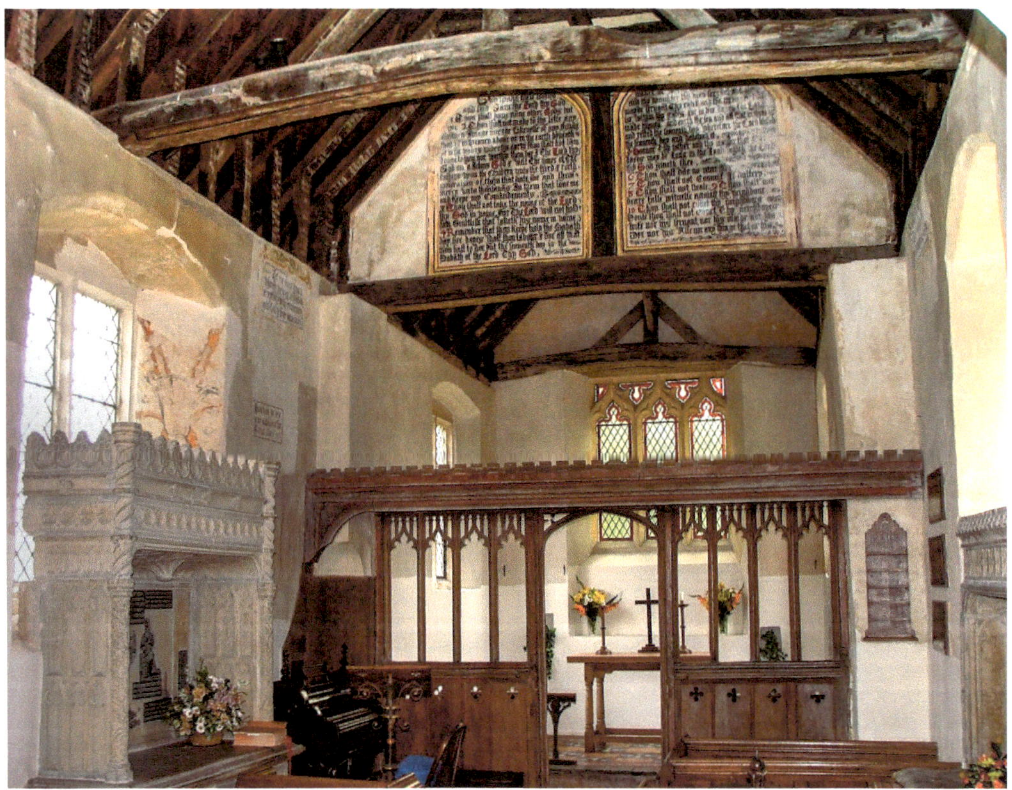

Burton. One of the most atmospheric small churches in Sussex. Medieval screen, tomb of William Goring and Decalogue high on the wall.

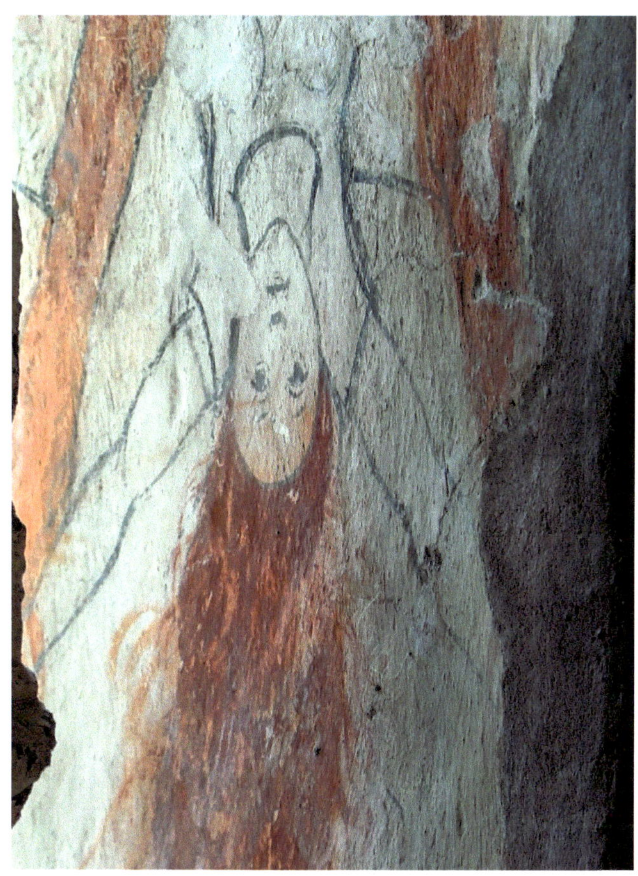

Burton. Medieval painting of a woman being crucified upside down. It may depict St Uncumber, a Portuguese princess.

them horizontally! Sir William was an important Tudor courtier who in his will left precious items that had been given to him by Anne of Cleves and Edward VI. On the south wall the painted royal arms of Charles I, dated 1636, are clear for all to see.

12. Chichester, St John's Chapel

The first-time visitor to this delightful building might wonder if it is an Anglican place of worship, for it looks unlike most Sussex churches. This is partly due to its date, 1812, and partly to its extreme evangelical use where the building was purely a box for the preaching of the word. It is also one of a rare breed – a proprietary chapel, erected by Trustees as a financial investment and without a parish of its own. Attendees would have belonged to one of the six parish churches in the city but, for whatever reason, paid to attend services here. The majority would have attended because of the reputation of the preachers, but some will have come because of the social status it gave them in the locality. Sadly, the finances were always rocky and for most of its history the chapel struggled to pay its way. It is slightly set back from the street, which makes it hard to find, but its handsome façade still makes a contribution to the 'New Town' quarter. Like the neighbouring houses it is built of local brick with a Portland stone pepperpot turret and Roman cement surrounds to

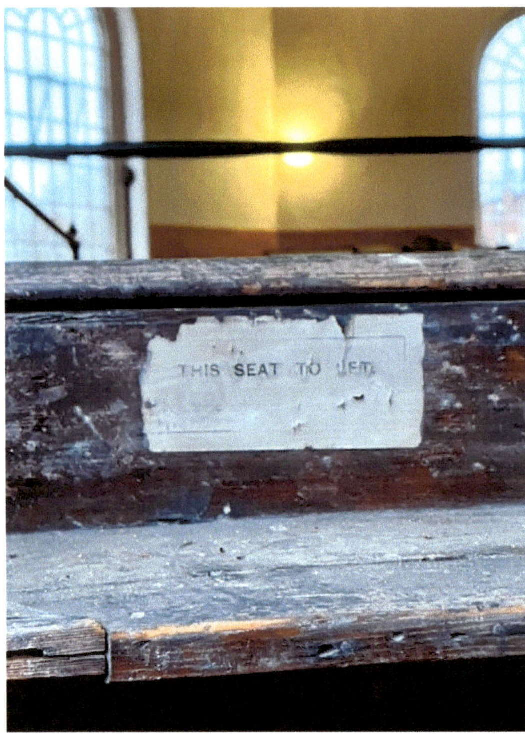

Chichester, St John's Chapel. As a proprietary chapel the only income came from pew rents. This notice in the gallery advertises that this seat is available. (Image by Stephen Riley)

its three west doors. The large door gave access to the body of the church where free seats were available; the other two led to staircases which took attendees to the rented seats in the galleries. In the 1851 Census of Religious Worship, it could seat 450 in free seats and 500 in rented seats. Inside, the focal point is the tall three-decker pulpit on a barley twist stem which totally hides the Holy Table behind with its reredos of the Decalogue, the Creed and the Lord's Prayer. The absence of a font shows that this was never a parish church, and there are only two memorials because burials were not allowed here either. In 1879 the ground floor was given the benches we see today, but the seating in the gallery has remained unaltered and even displays a nineteenth-century label advertising 'this seat to let'. To see upstairs an appointment should be made with the Friends of St John's who care for the chapel and who open the ground floor daily.

13. Church Norton, St Wilfrid's Chapel

This corner of the Manhood Peninsula attracts birdwatchers and those in search of the curious. It is very much a place apart – if you like a 'thin place' in modern parlance. St Wilfrid landed here in AD 681, bringing Christianity to the people of Sussex. Here too he founded a cathedral which was to be the seat of twenty-five successive bishops until their throne was moved to Chichester in 1075. After that, with a reduced status, the site of the cathedral became a parish church and part of this is what people see today, in its enormous churchyard. Today's chapel dates from the thirteenth century and was the chancel of a much larger church, the nave of which can be seen re-erected in today's parish church at Selsey, to which place it was removed in 1864. The limewashed exterior of the chapel is how most Sussex churches would have looked in the medieval period, the outer protection preventing the driving rain from penetrating the rubble walls. Inside this tiny building there is one big surprise – a sixteenth-century monument to John and Agatha Lewis. Following the Reformation, images of saints were declared illegal and mostly destroyed, but here is a graphic depiction of the martyrdom of St Agatha who was killed in Sicily by having her breasts removed. An image of St George also survives and I would think that it probably owes its survival to its isolated location. The east window contains glass by Heaton, Butler and Bayne of 1921 commemorating the Wingfield family who are depicted as St Michael, St Faith and St George, their medieval costumes amusingly contrasting with their photographic portraits. Other twentieth-century windows of importance include one depicting the wildlife of the area by Michael Farrar-Bell (1982) and another showing the role of women in nursing by Carl Edwards (1973). Artists and poets have always been drawn here. The writer R. C. Sherriff (*Journey's End*) came here to recover from his experiences in the First World War and his ashes are buried in the churchyard. In 1921 Rudyard Kipling visited and wrote a famous Christmas poem ('Eddi of Manhood End') which he set here in the seventh century.

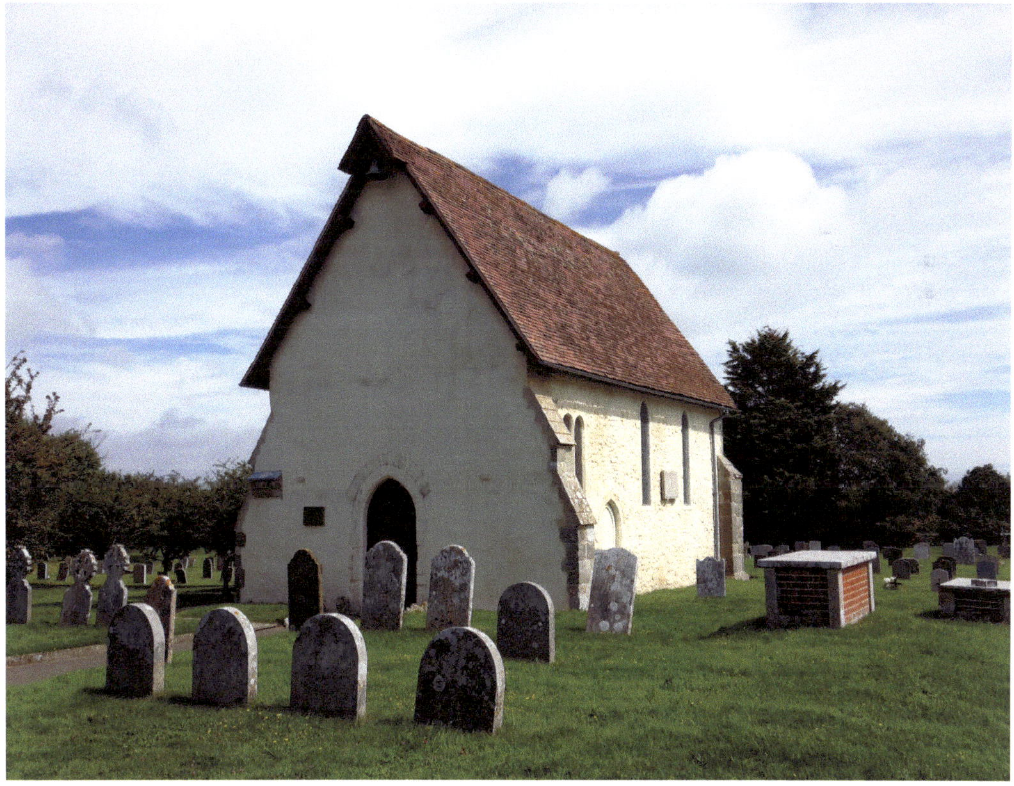

Church Norton. All that remains of the medieval successor to the first cathedral for Sussex is this thirteenth-century chancel. Note the traditional limewashed exterior.

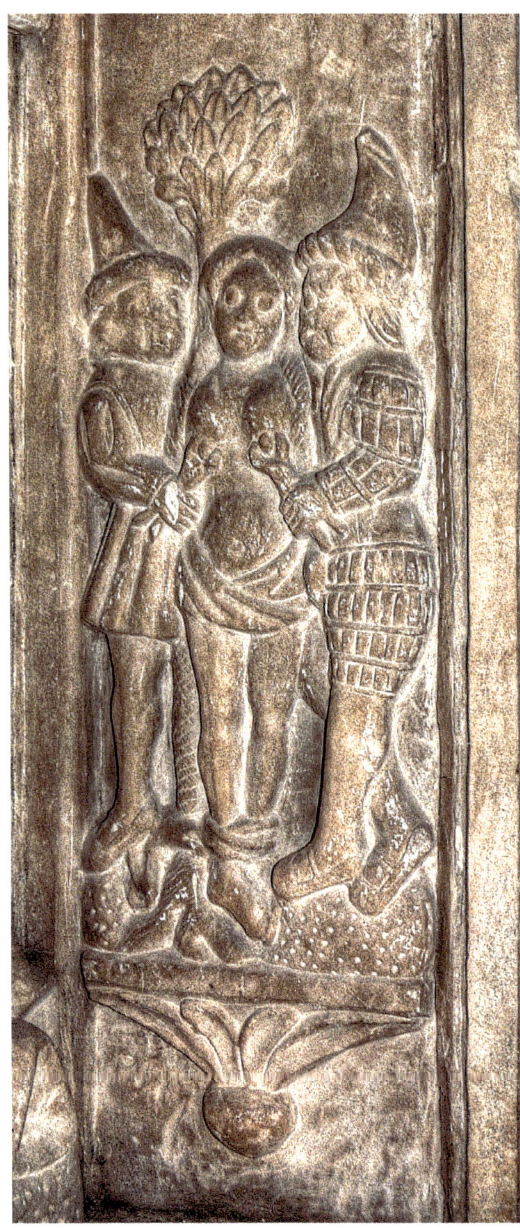

Church Norton. The grisly
martyrdom of St Agatha as depicted
on the mid-sixteenth-century tomb of
John and Agatha Lewis.

14. CLAPHAM, ST MARY

Not very easy to find but well worth the effort to see the nineteenth-century work
introduced by Sir Gilbert Scott into a simple thirteenth-century Downland church.
It can be a dark interior, so look for the light switches to appreciate the richness
of the Victorian fittings, especially the tiled reredos which is by William Morris. It
depicts archangels against a pattern of willows, roses, grapes and apples and is one

of just a handful he produced. Of the same period are the tiled floor, pulpit, chancel gates and stained glass. It all goes to create a magnificent ensemble. However, the church contains several older items of interest, particularly the monuments to the Shelley family. On the north wall of the chancel, and hard to miss, is the canopied wall monument of Sir William Shelley (d. 1548). He kneels with his seven sons, and his wife with their seven daughters. Unusually they all face east rather than each other, and one of the daughters wears the habit of a nun, even though by this late date all the monasteries had been closed. I wonder if she had died a nun, or if not what she went on to do? Above the figures are three circular shields of arms and higher still is a pediment with arabesque heads and a clumpy pendant which protrudes from a foliate head. At the rear of the church is a board recording a grant of £25 from the Incorporated Church Building Society towards the restoration of the building in 1872 which uncovered a blocked Norman window above the north arcade.

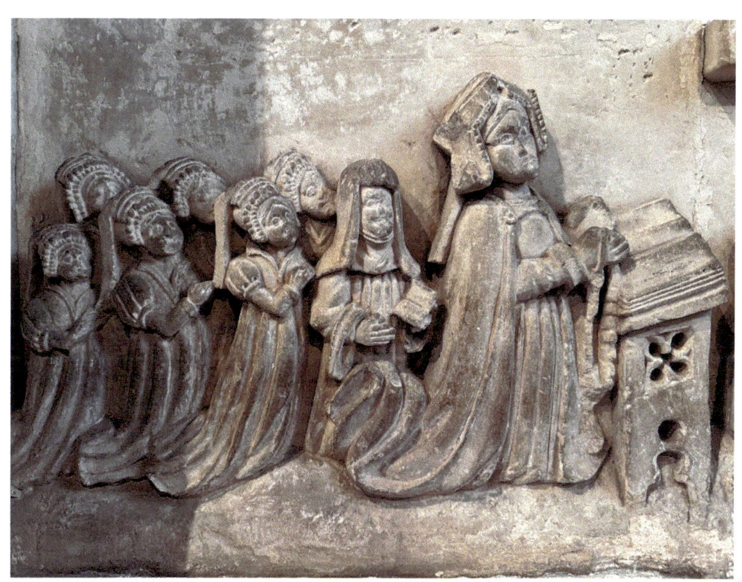

Right: Clapham. Lady Shelley kneels at a prayer desk and tells her rosary with her daughters, dating from the mid-sixteenth century. Unusually the eldest daughter is dressed as a nun.

Below: Clapham. An early work by William Morris, this tiled reredos relies more on the different foliages and fruits behind as much as on the four angels.

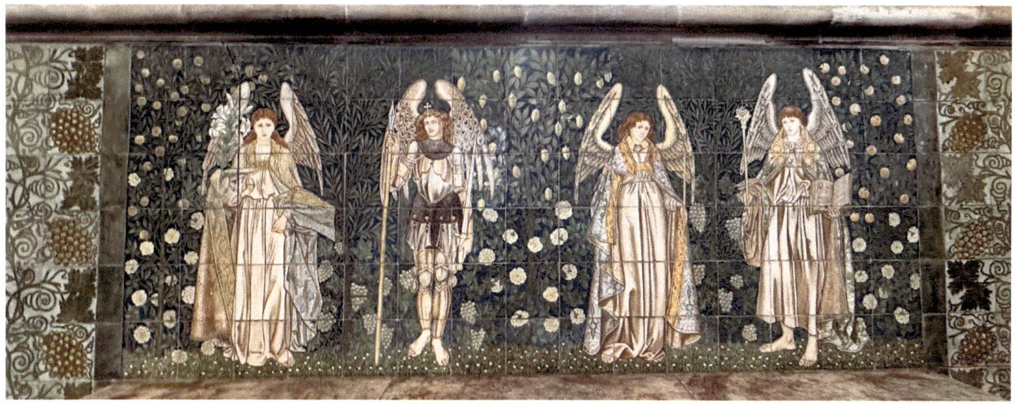

15. CLAYTON, ST JOHN THE BAPTIST

In the lee of the South Downs, Clayton church is a good example of a two-cell building of the eleventh century. In the absence of identifiable work, these buildings are hard to date exactly, and it may be just before or just after the Norman Conquest, although the height of its walls would suggest the former. The church is reached via a path of wavey stone which was formed under the sea and which has retained its ripples. One enters via the north door (covered in rusty nails as a result of hundreds of years' worth of public notices being displayed on it) and step down into an interior richly furnished with wall paintings. In 1093 the parish was given to Lewes Priory and it is likely that Cluniac monks came from there to create these works of art. Other Sussex churches in their gift were given a similar treatment, although the style of the paintings at Clayton is rather dissimilar to the others. Above the chancel arch is the risen Christ displaying the wounds on his hands – sat on a cushioned throne within a mandorla. To either side are the Apostles and along both north and south walls are processions. Luckily there are interpretation panels in the church, as some of the details are unclear, but the overall effect is stunning. My favourite section is towards the east end of the north wall where a six-sided building represents the New Jerusalem. A lower series of paintings is made up of separate scenes and is not as

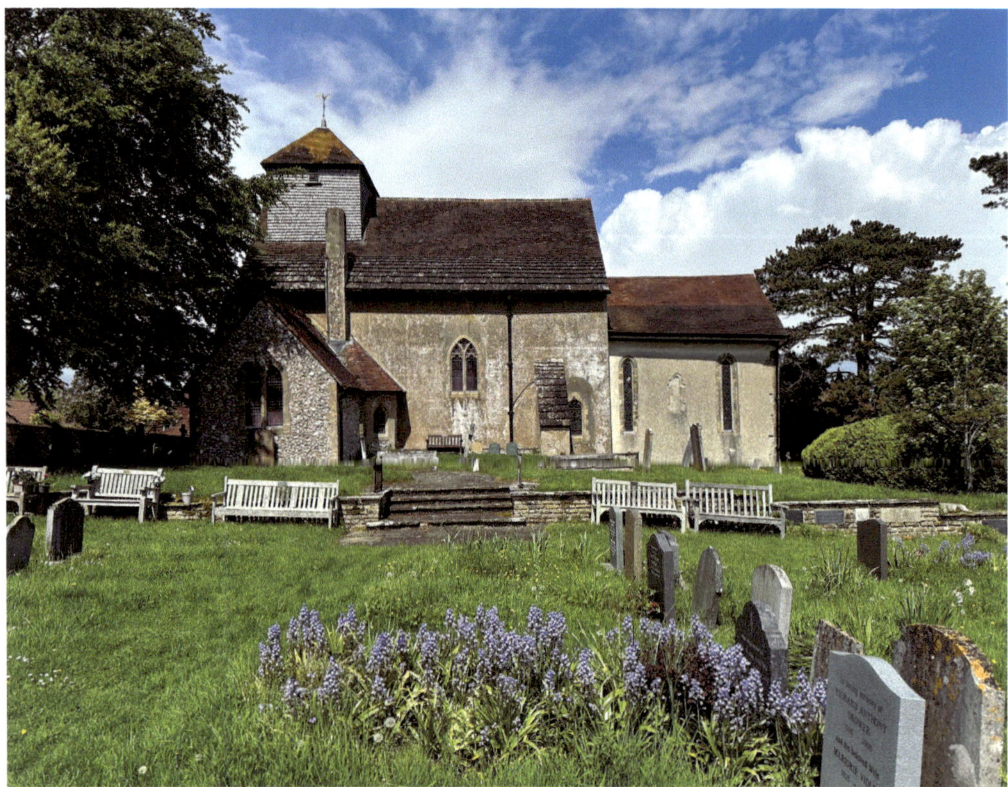

Clayton. Exterior from the south. The lower slope of the nave roof is covered with heavy Horsham slabs. Apart from the vestry the church retains its twelfth-century footprint.

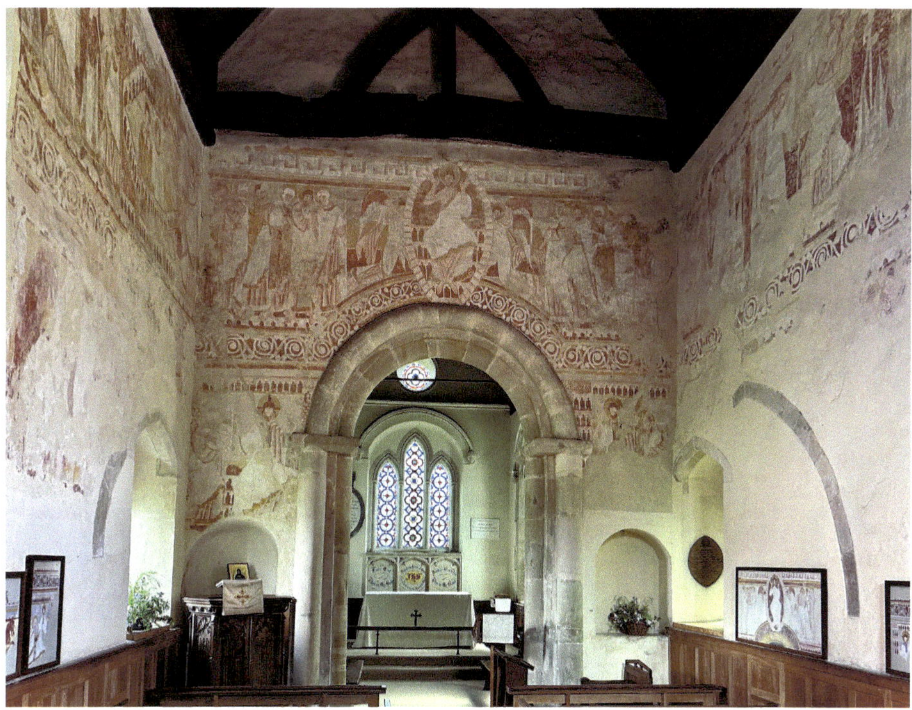

Clayton. Interior showing two levels of early wall paintings. The central figure depicts the Risen Christ sitting on a throne within a mandorla.

well preserved. At the Reformation the paintings were all limewashed over, which preserved them, and they were not uncovered until 1893. Sadly, today the church has an active bat colony and their droppings and urine are slowly damaging the paintings. In both the north and south walls of the nave are blocked arches which originally lead to chapels. The chancel has an altogether different feel to the nave as it was substantially remodelled by the Victorians. Mounted on the wall is one rather fine brass of Revd Richard Idon, priest, who died in 1523, depicted in eucharistic vestments, holding a chalice with wafer. In the churchyard, between the church and the road is the grave of Sir Norman Hartnell, most famous as the designer of Queen Elizabeth II's Coronation gown, and of the Queen Mother's extensive wardrobe.

16. DIDLING, ST ANDREW

This church could not be more straightforward, and that is its charm. It stands on the northern slope of the Downs, in splendid isolation and is known locally as 'The Shepherds' Church'. There may have been a small farming community here, but if so, it was very poor as records tell of financial problems almost from the start. Whilst this appears to be a single-cell building, there is a small set back between nave and chancel, although there is no change in roof structure. Nothing is earlier than the thirteenth century, and most of the windows are of this date. The east and west walls have been rebuilt and the old windows reinserted, whilst the exterior flint walls have been limewashed, as they would have originally been. The visitor steps into a totally

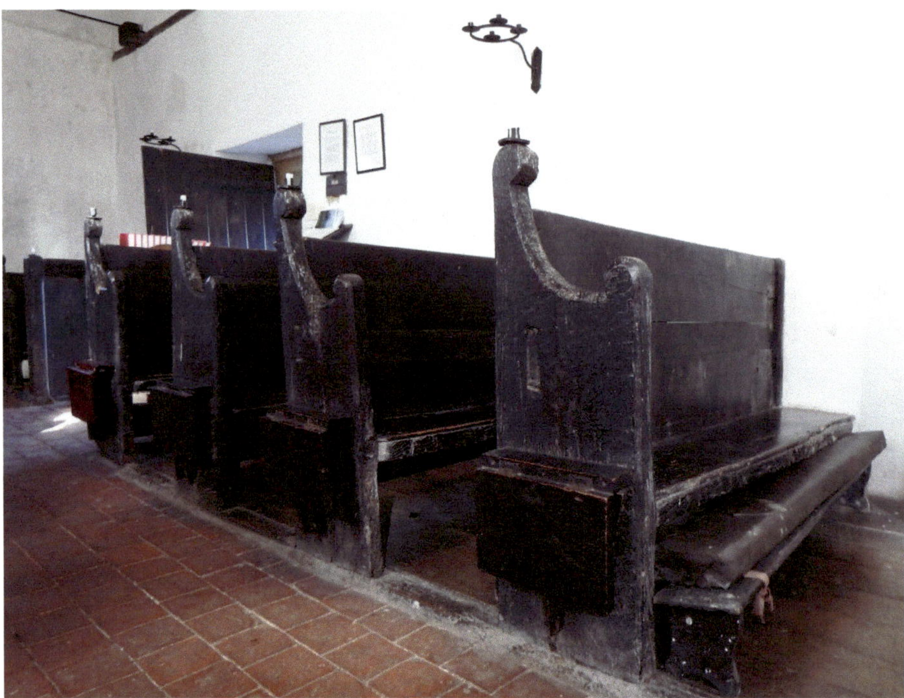

Didling. This simple country church is filled with very early wooden benches. The flaps on the end were added when Georgian gentlemen needed somewhere to place their top hats.

white interior, the plastered ceiling making up for the relatively small windows, all but one of which is a single light. The font is tub-shaped, of the type that is notoriously difficult to date, and could easily be early thirteenth century which would make it contemporary with the building. It might just be earlier, in which case it has been brought in from elsewhere. What we really come here to see are the wooden benches which are the oldest set in any Sussex church. In the gangway their ends are carved with a prominent 'elbow' which is typical of thirteenth-century work, though these are probably a hundred years later. At the other end they just slot into the wall, giving an unfinished appearance. Originally, they would have been open-backed and, of course, the flaps on the ends were added in the Georgian period for the gentlemen to rest their top hats!

17. EASTBOURNE, ST MARY

A showstopper of a church built to serve the village of 'Borne' from the late Norman period onwards. I am sure many visitors to the modern resort of Eastbourne don't know that this church even exists, a mile inland. Whilst there wasn't a settlement on the beach at the time of its construction, there was access by a stream which would have been used to bring Caen stone from Normandy up the valley to build the church. The visitor steps down into an extremely long building and it is immediately obvious that the nave and chancel were built on completely different alignments. This is usually because those charged with setting out the foundations used a different east

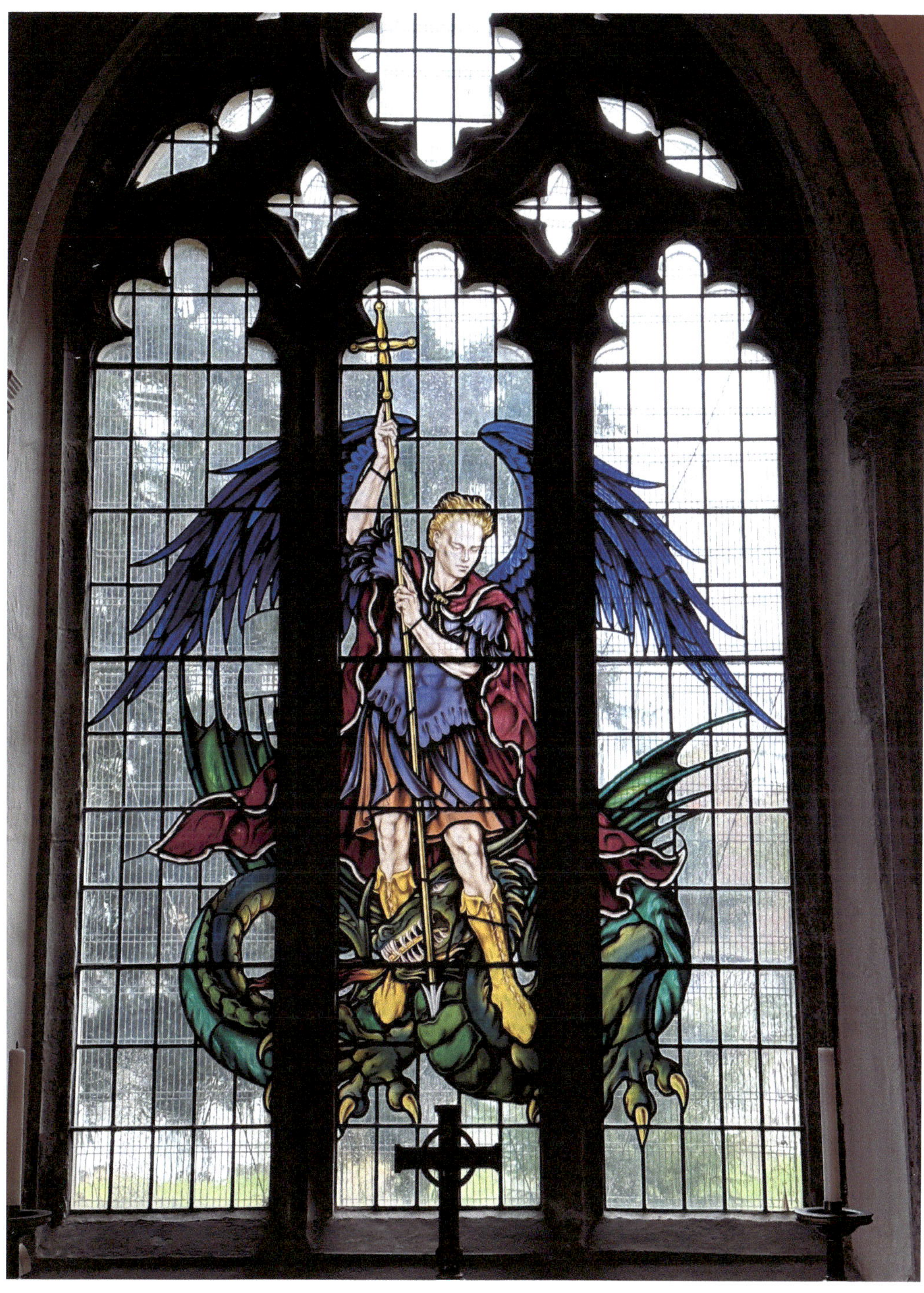

Eastbourne, St Mary. St Michael the Archangel in bold twentieth-century stained glass by the designer Hugh Easton.

line (calculated by watching where the sun rose). Almost the whole core of the church is of the late twelfth century and we are able to date its components by the carvings on the capitals and arches which vary slightly throughout the building. Only the west end of the nave is later and dates from the time when the tower was built in the late fourteenth century. The entrance stairway to the rood loft is to be found in the south aisle and you can clearly see the most unusual feature of the church – a thirteenth-century piscina high up by the chancel arch to show that there was an altar actually on top of the rood loft. Whilst the loft and screen have gone, the screens dividing the chancel from its chapels remain from the fourteenth century, as do the screens between the aisles and eastern chapels. The door in the east wall of the chancel leads to a medieval vestry, easier to see when outside. On the north side of the sanctuary is an Easter Sepulchre, a tomb that was specifically designed to be used as part of the Easter Liturgy which today houses a bronze angel designed by Sir Ninian Comper. The north chapel east window is an arresting design by Hugh Easton – notice his weathervane signature in the bottom right-hand corner. Here, too, is the large memorial to Elizabeth Gildredge and daughter, mostly inscribed in Latin but with an English poem composed by her husband. It is a feast of heraldry and sculpture, but

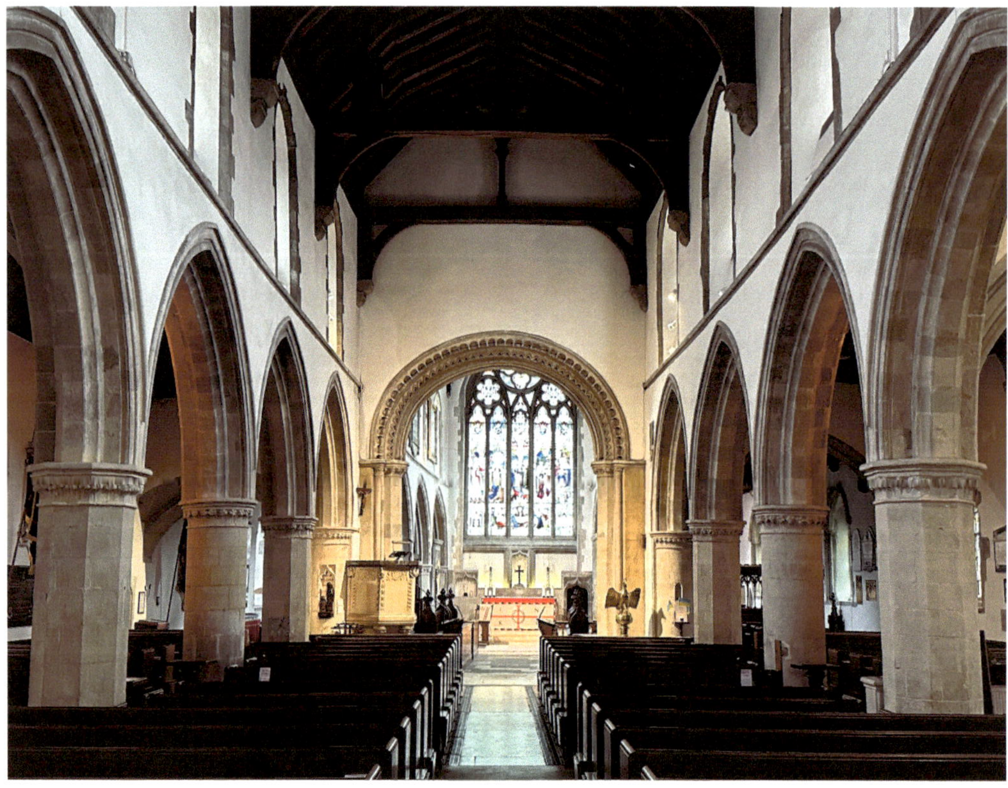

Eastbourne, St Mary. Interior looking east showing the massive Norman chancel arch and the round and octagonal piers of the thirteenth-century nave. It is clear to see that the nave and chancel are not in alignment.

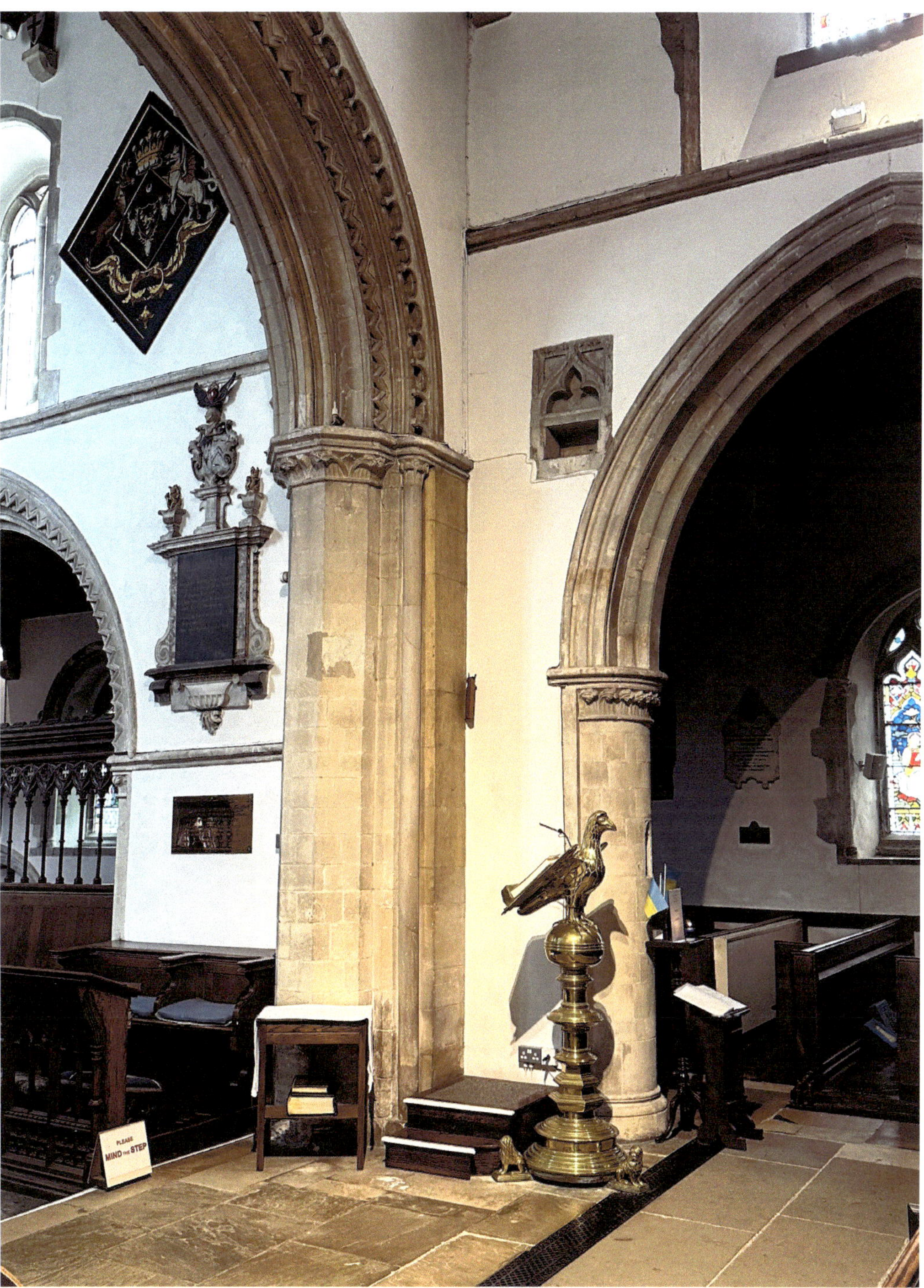

Eastbourne, St Mary. High in the wall, at the junction of nave and chancel, is a thirteenth-century piscina which shows that there was once an altar here, on top of the rood loft.

I always think the angels at the top look rather punch drunk! There are many other interesting memorials to detail in a visit. That to Mary Lushington (d. 1775), quite a conventional eighteenth-century tablet, is enlivened by an added inscription which tells it was moved by the vicar 'with the approbation' of the Lushington family in 1851. In the south aisle Henry Lushington's death in 1763 is described in lurid detail. He was imprisoned in the Black Hole of Calcutta in 1756 and survived only to be murdered in prison at Patna seven years later. The inscription triumphally tells us that in the course of his murder he was able to kill three of his guards.

18. EASTBOURNE, ST SAVIOUR

This enormous church of 1865 dominates the area between the station and the sea in a town which was developed as a seaside resort by the 7th Duke of Devonshire. Designed by one of the most famous nineteenth-century church architects, George Edmund Street, it was the gift of George Whelpton, whose money had come from 'Whelpton's Pills', a Victorian quack cure-all. One of the conditions of his gift was that his clergyman son should be the first incumbent. The church stands on a corner site and is built of polychromatic brickwork with stone dressings and spire. The tower is almost detached from the nave, and this isn't the only architectural curiosity

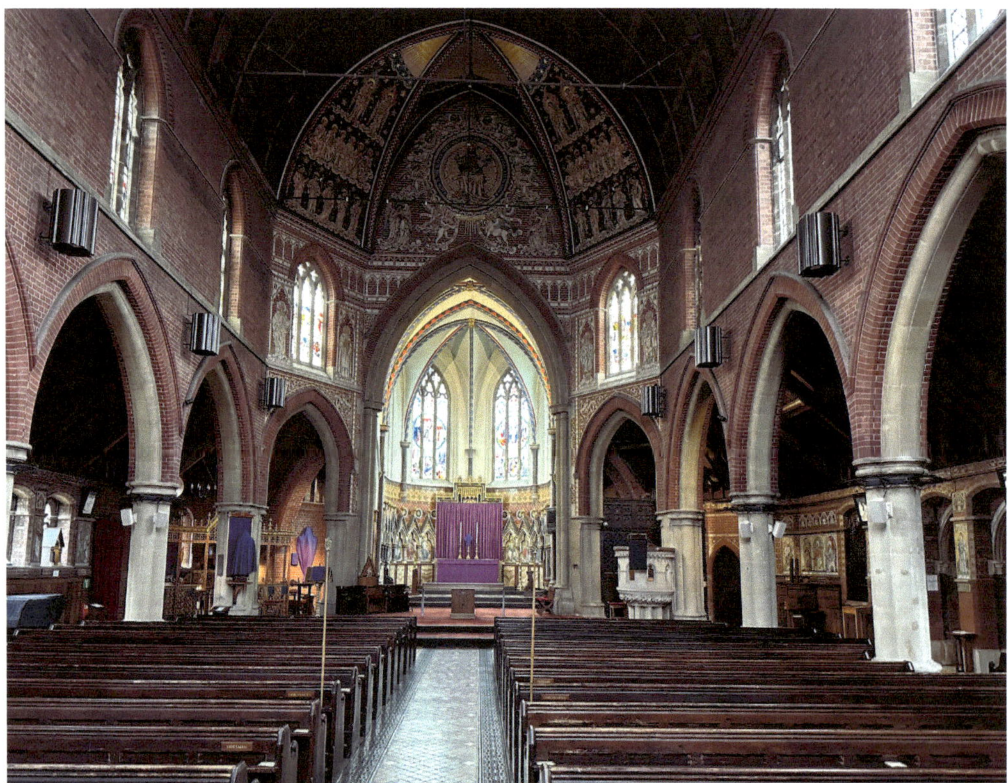

Eastbourne, St Saviour. Interior of 1865 by George Edmund Street with the unusual, canted junction of nave and chancel.

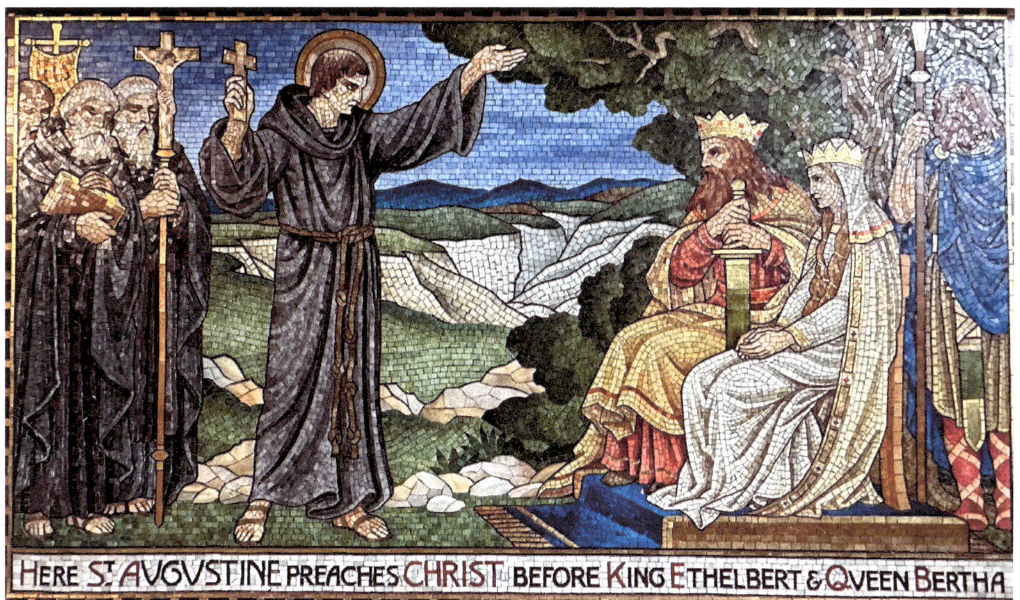

Eastbourne, St Saviour. A rather stern St Augustine has an audience of King Ethelbert and Queen Bertha of Kent in one of a series of mosaic panels.

for inside the east end of the nave is canted to lead the eye into the much narrower apsidal chancel. It is a very successful device, especially as the recent nave altar now sits in a space that looks like it was created for it. The walls and ceiling here are decorated by the firm of Clayton and Bell, representing subjects including Christ in Majesty surrounded by the Host of Heaven, including Martyrs, Apostles, Angels and the Doctors of the Church. Throughout the church are mosaic panels made by Salviati and Powell's. I especially like the panel by the font depicting St Ethelbert and Queen Bertha, rulers of Kent when St Augustine arrived in AD 597. The reredos to the High Altar dates from the twentieth century and was designed by Randoll Blacking, whose work is always worth seeking out. As a pupil of the much more famous Ninian Comper he delighted in setting his statues under gilded Gothic canopies of fifteenth-century Netherlandish inspiration. It makes an interesting comparison to Street's much simpler Early English form of Gothic used throughout the church.

19. EAST GULDEFORD, ST MARY

Only separated from Kent by a watery dyke, St Mary's is quite unlike any other English church. It was almost the last complete medieval church to be built in Sussex and takes the form of a brick rectangle standing on land reclaimed from the sea by Sir Richard Guldeford in the late 1400s. Sir Richard was an important player at Court, and a Knight of the Garter (his Garter plate survives at St George's Chapel, Windsor) and used the money earned from his positions to reclaim the last area of the Walland Marshes from the sea. As the new land became habitable, he obtained permission to found this church to serve it in 1499. His building is about as pared down as it is possible to get, and it is quite believable that some people drive past this church without recognising it as such for the exterior looks rather like an expensive barn, entirely built of brick, with huge buttresses at the west end. The weathervane is formed of a shepherd's crook and a tiny lamb, whilst the roof is made up of two separate gabled structures which would suggest to the visitor that the interior is divided by an arcade, but surprisingly you walk into a single, flat-ceilinged hall. The wide gangway suggests there was formerly a series of supports for the roof. Internally the only division of the space into a nave and chancel is achieved by early nineteenth-century pierced spandrels under the tie beam, but there must once have been a rood screen at this point. Surprisingly, the church has a Norman font of common design which must have been brought here from another church. At each corner is a moulding that shows that it originally stood on columns, rather than on the present rather dumpy plinth. Like many Marsh churches the floors are of brick. On the north wall is a carved stone armorial of the Guldeford family whilst in the chancel are four angel corbels which would originally have been painted. After only a couple of generations, they fell foul of the iconoclasts. Apart from that the fittings are all of a later date including box

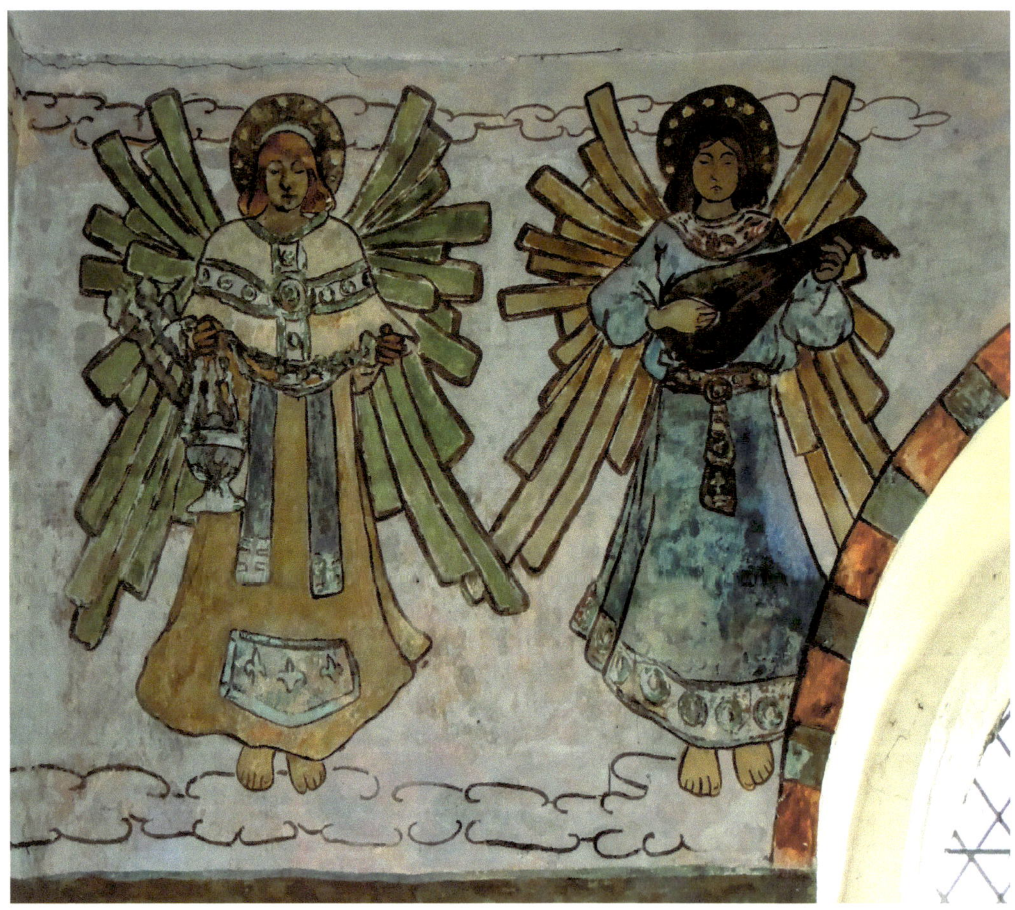

East Guldeford. These Edwardian Arts and Crafts angels were added to the simple sixteenth-century interior to give it a more ecclesiastical feel. (Image by Simon Knott)

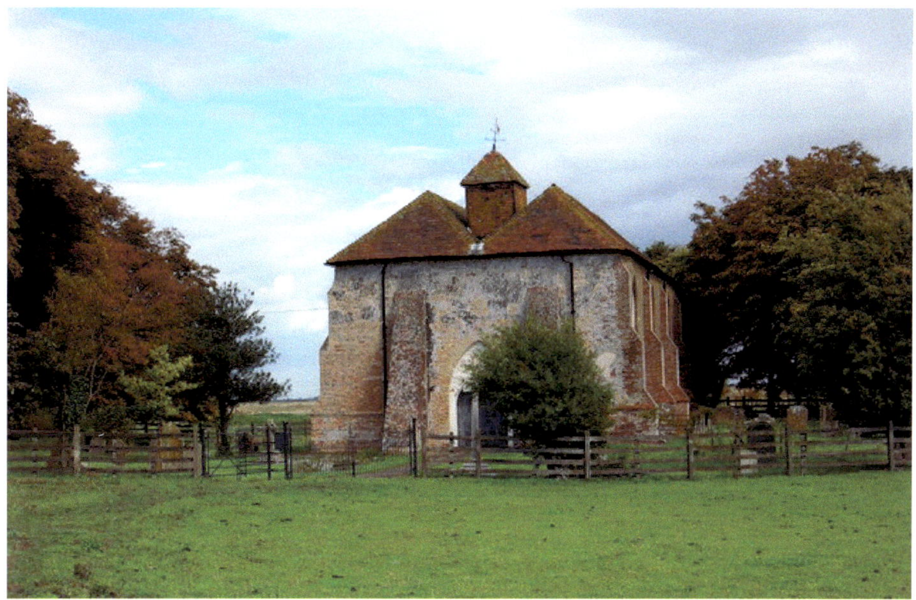

East Guldeford. The brick exterior from the west showing its double-hipped roof and views across the Romney Marshes behind. (Image by Julian P. Guffog)

pews, Decalogue and royal arms of George IV. Dominating the east end are some charming naïve paintings of angels dating from the Edwardian period which add some much-needed colour to an otherwise clinical interior. Sadly, Sir Richard Guldeford died on pilgrimage to the Holy Land in 1506, shortly after the consecration of the church in which he might have expected to be buried, and he was instead buried in Jerusalem.

20. FLETCHING, ST ANDREW AND ST MARY THE VIRGIN

It is always a delight to visit this village church as it contains a wide variety of features to interest the visitor. The outside is a textbook study in the use of local stone. The tower is Norman, built in rubble stone with prominent bell openings of the period. Later, buttresses were added to the corners and these are in ashlar blocks, the stone having been cut and laid more regularly. The porch is ashlar too, whilst the south transept wall is of rubble but completely unlike the Norman tower in its coarsed layers. When you walk round to the north side there is a surprise waiting for you because the north transept is double the length of the south. It has clearly been extended, in this case for the mausoleum of the 1st Earl of Sheffield (d. 1821). Much of the church is roofed in local Horsham slab stone. The nave is mainly thirteenth century with circular piers, with heightened walls and a fourteenth-century clerestory. The interesting parts are the transepts. The north transept north wall has a simple wooden door which leads into the mausoleum – which you can already see through the original window above. This is an odd structure as the wall is built so close to the door that it is almost impossible to read the lugubrious inscription! It's also interesting to read that the historian Edward Gibbon, a friend of Lord Sheffield, is also buried within. In the transept is a delightful window of

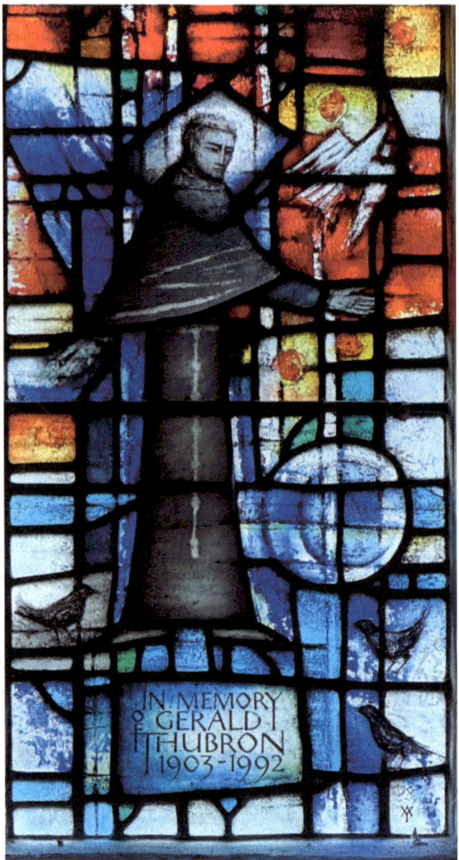

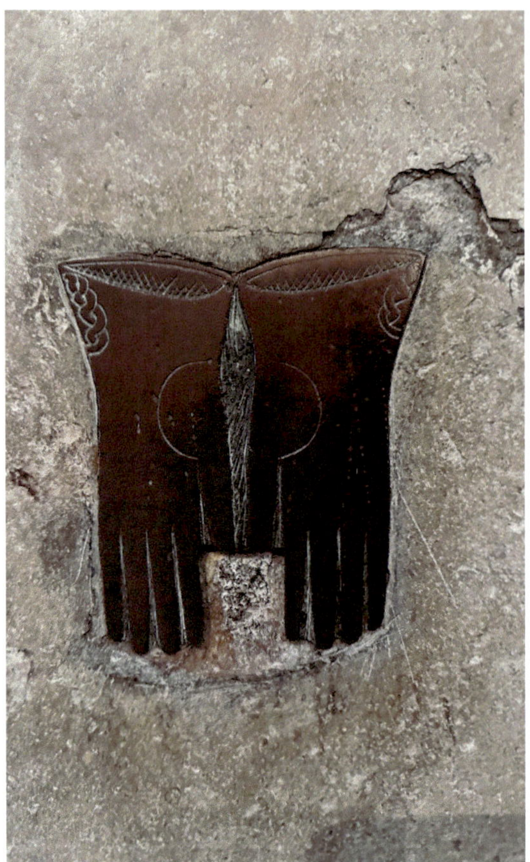

Above left: Fletching. Twentieth-century stained glass by Alan Younger depicting St Francis of Assisi.

Above right: Fletching. An unusual representation on a Sussex brass of a medieval profession, in this case a glove maker.

1992 by Alan Younger, depicting St Francis. As you leave the transepts look high above you at two examples of funeral armour, carried at heraldic funerals in the seventeenth and eighteenth centuries. Their use was replaced by the carrying of hatchments, or shields of arms painted on canvas panels, examples of which also survive in the church. In contrast to the sombre north transept, the south is full of treasures. The large alabaster monument is to Richard Leche, High Sheriff, who died in 1596. Next to it, and easy to miss is an upright slab inset with two brasses. One carries the inscription, the other is of a pair of gloves showing that the deceased, Peter Denot, was a glove maker. A much larger brass is on a table tomb against the south wall and depicts two members of the fourteenth-century Dalyngrigge family of Bodiam Castle. Behind is their crest, a unicorn's head. In front of the tomb chest is a delightful mini effigy of a husband and wife which must have come from elsewhere. Both effigies retain significant traces of their original colour. It would be lovely to know their identities.

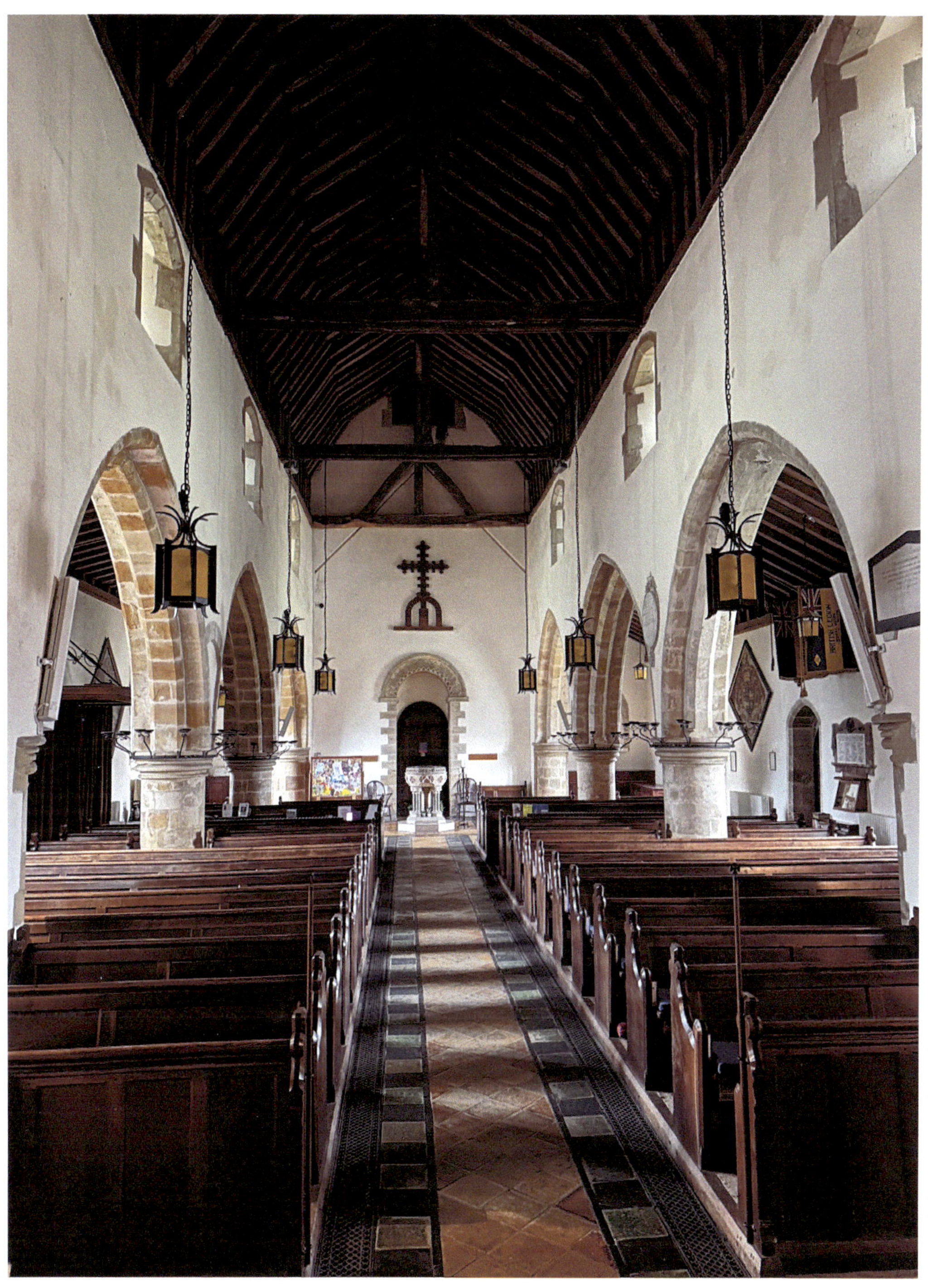

Fletching. This view of the nave looking west shows the original roofline scar on the tower, before the clerestory windows were added in the fourteenth century.

21. GLYNDE, ST MARY THE VIRGIN

Many estate churches play a vital visual role in the parkland of a country house, but here at Glynde the church built in 1763 sits next to the stables of Glynde Place, on the site of its medieval predecessor. It was built for the landowner, Richard Trevor, Bishop of Durham, and takes the form of a simple preaching box. Simple it may be, but expensively done. The architect was Sir Thomas Robinson, a northern gentleman-architect who had already designed a similar church for his own country estate at Rokeby, in Teesdale. There he had used local sandstone but here on the edge of the Sussex Downs he used flint with Portland stone dressings. The west front is particularly effective, with the flints being closely knapped into rectangles and laid in horizontal courses. We know the name of the Master Mason who worked on it, John Morris of Lewes, together with the names of some of his craftsmen. Above the west door is a tremendous shield of arms of Bishop Trevor, surmounted by his mitre, giving the parishioners no doubt as to whom they should be grateful for such a luxurious building. The dentilled eaves and gables are far more elaborate than at Rokeby, being formed of timber rather than stone. The interior of the church is a great surprise – the walls being hung with printed hessian and the ceiling looking as if it has been dropped in from the mansion next door. The church is filled with box pews, although they are not in their original configuration for the interior was altered by the Victorians in order to make it more ecclesiologically correct with a focus on the Holy Table. This latter was set into a recess in the east wall. At Rokeby the church was even more

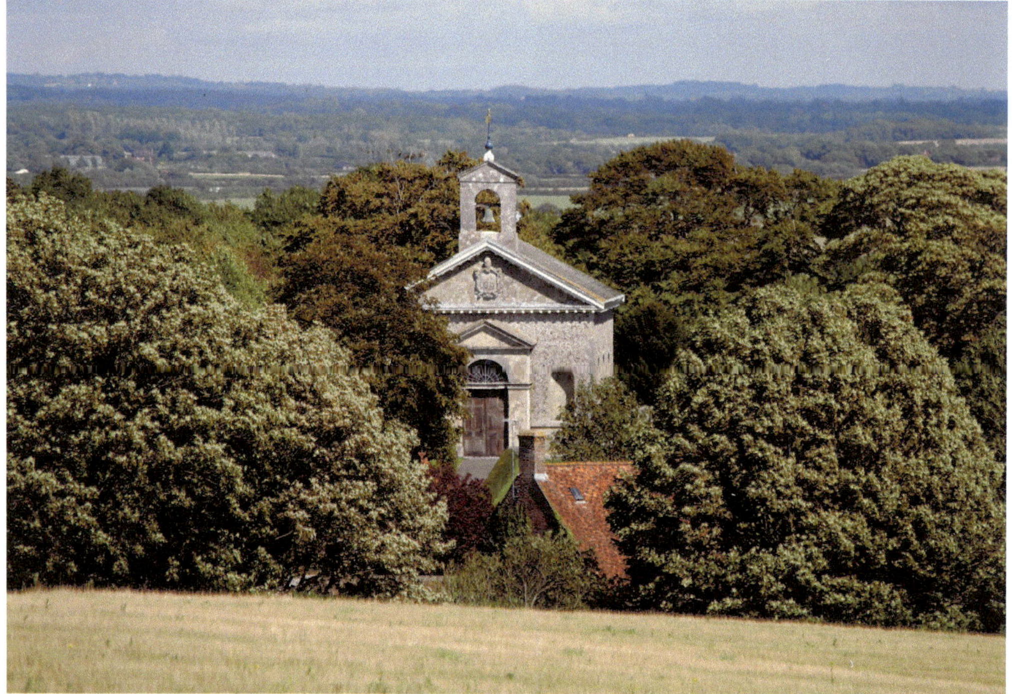

Glynde. The most unexpected Georgian church in Sussex, in a rural setting next to Glynde Place. (Image by Mark Wordington)

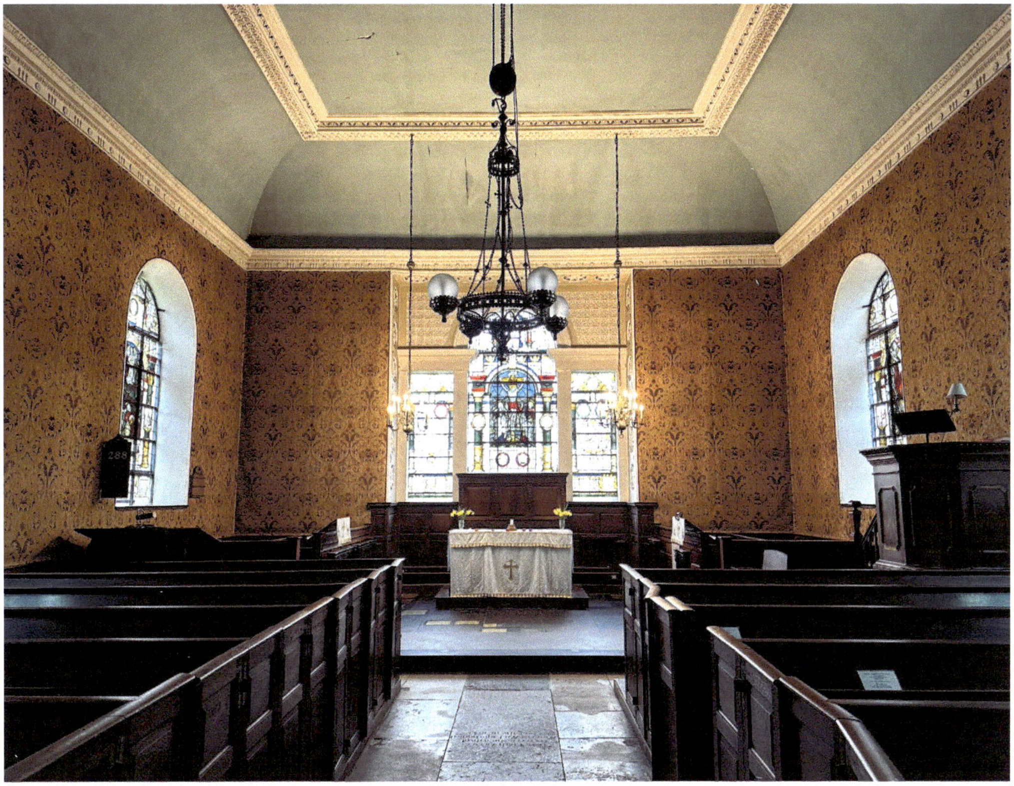

Glynde. The inside walls are hung with printed hessian which, added to the decorative plaster ceiling, creates a very domestic feel to the interior.

Glynde. Owing to lack of space the earlier ledgerstones of the Trevor family have been usurped by their successors the Brands in order to be memorialised as patrons of the church.

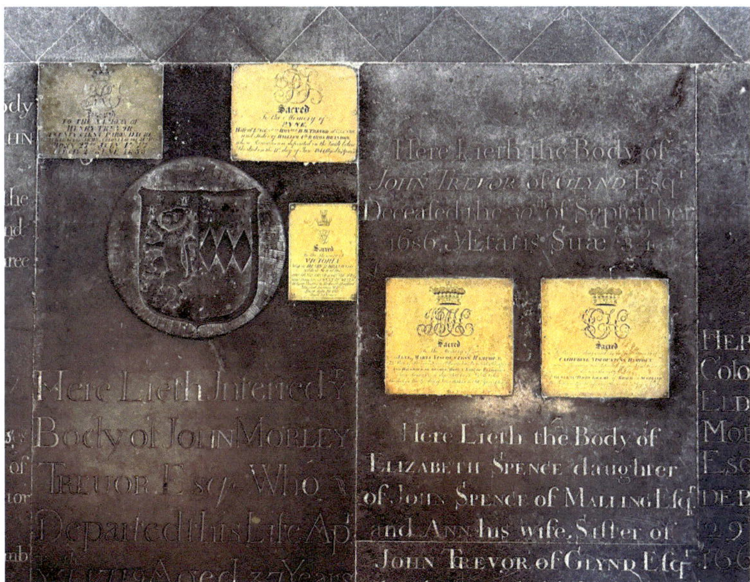

altered by the Victorians by the addition of a chancel.) There are seven stained-glass windows by Charles Eamer Kempe, the well-known Sussex-born artist, installed from 1894 onwards. Kempe had been much influenced by medieval Flemish designs, so he must have been delighted to have been asked to incorporate many sixteenth- and seventeenth-century Netherlandish panels in his designs. My 'favourite' is the hanging of an unknown saint by being thrown down a well – but do take binoculars! There are further Netherlandish glass panels in the hall and on the staircase landing in Glynde Place. In front of the altar are the ledger stones to the Trevor family. When they ran out of space for new ledgers, they set coffin plates into the ledgers of their ancestors which now form a most interesting pavement of genealogical interest.

22. Herstmonceux, All Saints

Famed for its castle which lies just a field away, Herstmonceux also boasts a fine church, reached down a long lane from the village. The churchyard wall includes a mounting block, showing that many worshippers would have come to church on horseback. The south aisle and nave are under a single roof structure known as a 'catslide', which is quite a common Sussex feature. This frequently makes the interior dark but here characterful wooden dormer windows of nineteenth-century date solve the problem. The west doorway has been blocked in and within the infill may be found a Harmer terracotta plaque, in the form of a boldly signed urn. Inside, the north capitals are of unique thirteenth-century designs, each one different to its neighbour, whilst on the south side of the sanctuary is the eighteenth-century Decalogue with a brilliantly painted IHS in a sunburst at the top. It is unusual to find these at a height to see clearly, but this has been moved from the east wall. We have really come here for the amazing monument that stands between the chancel and north chapel and to discover its complicated history. It certainly is the most colourful monument in the county, having been repainted in the 1970s. Today the two effigies commemorate the 8th Lord Dacre (d. 1533) and his son Thomas Fiennes who predeceased him. However, the style of the armour is not of that date and it is thought that these two figures were purchased when Battle Abbey was being demolished following its dissolution

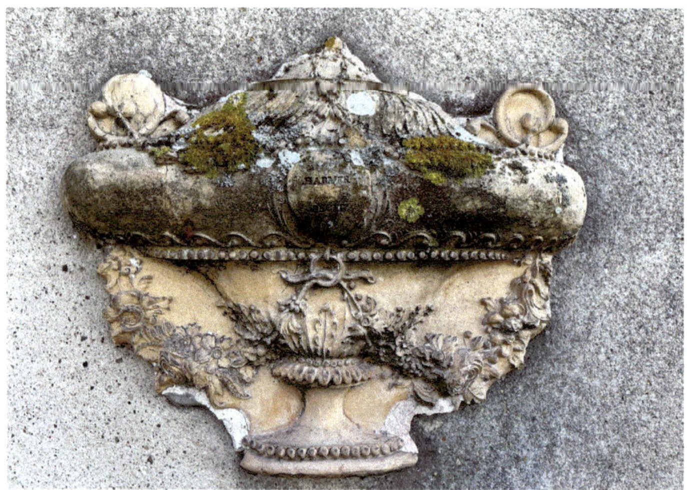

Herstmonceux. Set into the west wall is a Harmer Plaque, one of dozens in the county produced by an enterprising family of Heathfield potters. It is clearly signed.

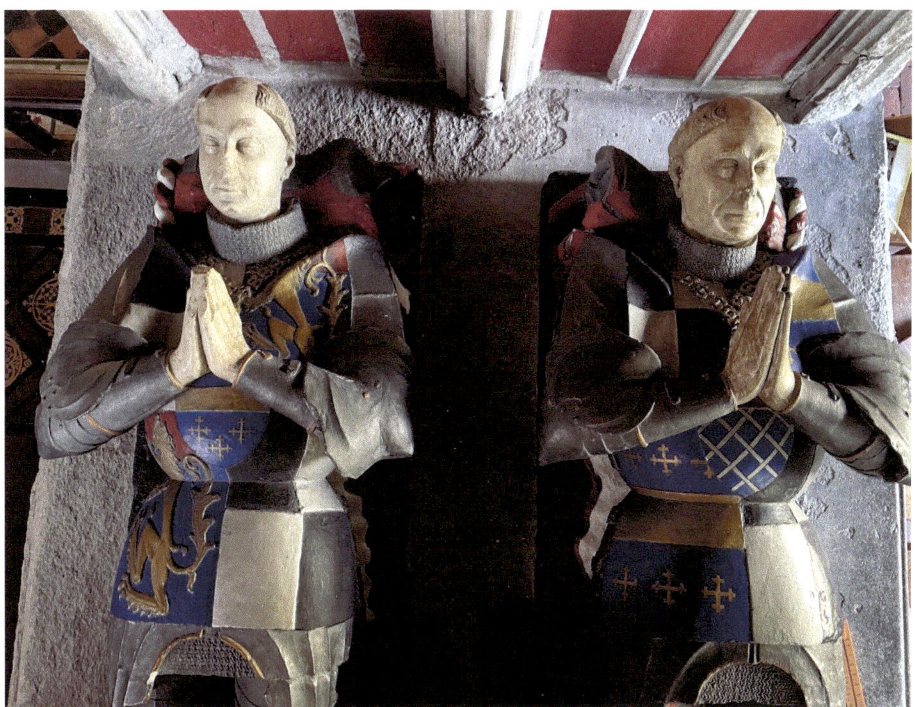

Herstmonceux. These effigies were originally in Battle Abbey and were reused here to commemorate members of the Dacre family in the sixteenth century.

and then reused by the Dacre family who were short of money and probably couldn't afford to commission a new monument. If this supposition is correct, it is probable that the effigies originally belonged to Lord Hoo and Hastings (d. 1455) and his half-brother Thomas. Lord Hoo was a powerful courtier and soldier who acted as a diplomat between England and France and helped negotiate the marriage of Henry VI to Margaret of Anjou. A prayer book he commissioned is now in the collection of the Royal Irish Academy and contains a picture of him and his wife. The tomb chest itself is also older but was probably always in this church and was installed when the north chapel was added by the Fiennes family in the middle of the fifteenth century. The chapel is built of the same bricks as the castle, making an interesting coupling.

23. Horsted Keynes, St Giles

Set away from the village green, St Giles is one of those churches which hides its Norman core until you get inside. The exterior appears to be all thirteenth and fourteenth century, dominated by a crossing tower with needle-like spire. On the south side of the chancel is a prominent blocked arch, the only trace of a former south chapel. Like many other sandstone churches, it is quite easy to see where alterations have been made, from the different ways in which the stone has been used. Inside you can see at a glance work of three different periods. The far arch under the tower, into the chancel, is Norman, as are its two companions. The nave arcade is thirteenth century, with circular piers, whilst the east nave tower arch, the tallest

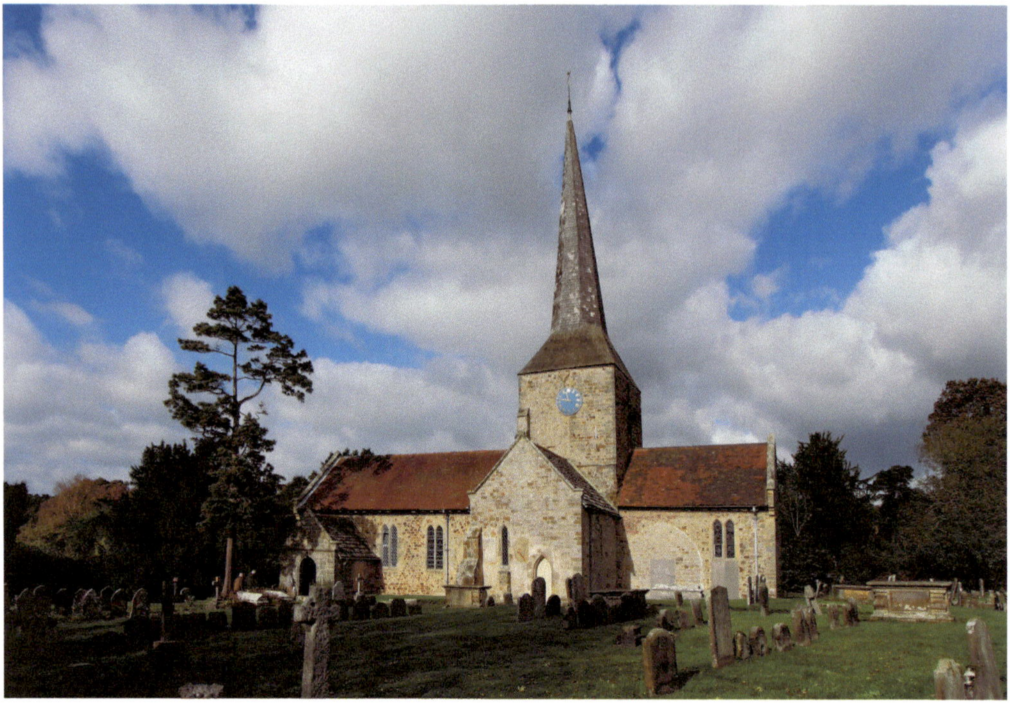

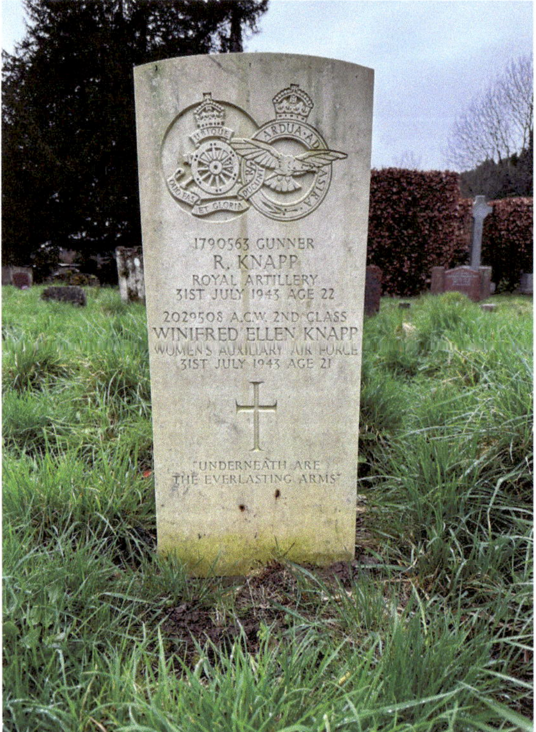

Above: Horsted Keynes. Exterior from the south. The building hides its Norman origins well, but not the former south chapel, the blocked arch of which dominates the south chancel wall.

Left: This Commonwealth War Grave remembers Winifred and Ronald Knapp who were killed on their wedding day whilst on leave from active service.

of them all, is fourteenth century. It is very clear by the abrupt vertical edges on the outer face where the medieval rood screen and loft stood. Within an arched recess in the chancel is another medieval miniature effigy (see also Fletching). This time it is of a cross-legged knight and dates from the thirteenth century. Long thought of as Crusaders' effigies, we now know this is not the case and that crossed-legged figures were designed to make the effigy appear more lifelike. In the churchyard are two interesting graves. Enclosed by a beech hedge to the east of the church are the graves of former Prime Minister Harold Macmillan (d. 1986) and his family. Nearby is a single Commonwealth War Grave, unusual for the fact that the grave contains two people. Here lie Mr and Mrs Knapp tragically killed on their wedding day during the Second World War whilst on leave from military service. They were walking home along the railway line after the reception when they were struck by a train.

24. HOVE, ST ANDREW, WATERLOO STREET

In the decade from 1810 Brighton and Hove became the fastest-growing populations in the country. The establishment of the Royal Pavilion made the area famous, and wealthy families came here for the season – all requiring accommodation. This saw an increased growth in all service industries, including places of worship. St Andrew's was built in 1827 as a proprietary chapel to serve the new Brunswick Estate where Hove and Brighton meet. It was designed by the young Charles Barry, later to become famous as architect of the Palace of Westminster and paid for by the Revd Edward Everard. You had to pay to attend services here and pew rents provided the owner with an income, together with income from burials within its vaults. This made sure

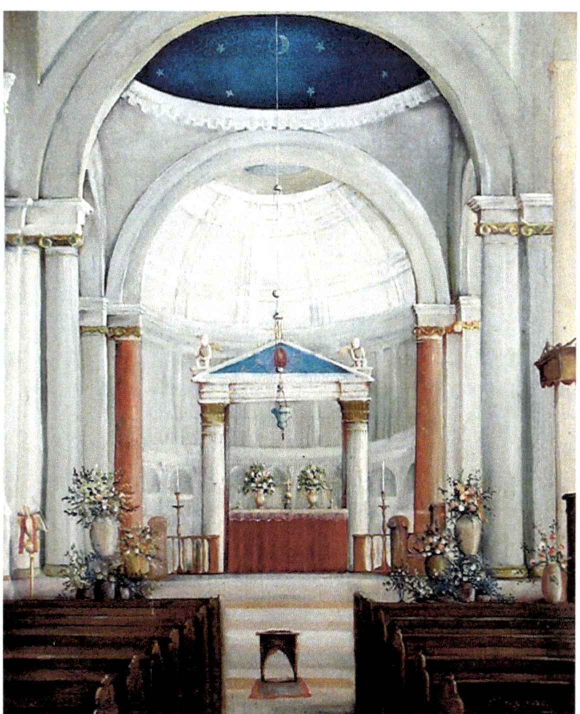

Hove, St Andrew, Waterloo Street. In the early twentieth century the vicar attempted to make this church interior 'like a little piece of Italy'.

that the attendees could be certain to only mix with their peers who were further
segregated by having their own entrance doors and staircase. It became the church
of choice for visiting royalty and their attendant dukes and duchesses. The front
facing Waterloo Street is of Portland stone ashlar but if you look down the side
you'll see that the church is built of stock brick – just like the grand houses it served.
The interior was altered in the late Victorian period and again in the early twentieth
century to create what the priest at the time called 'a little piece of Italy in Waterloo
Street'. The stained-glass figures in the south wall are set into what are known
as Venetian roundels and are by the firm of Hardman and Co., whilst in the east
vestibule is an amazing window of the Annunciation by Christopher Webb. There
are two good memorials by the royal sculptor John Ternouth including one to Lord
Charles Somerset (d. 1831), the first occupant of the vaults below. Unbelievably,
attendees were still paying pew rents into the 1960s and eventually the church closed.
It is now cared for by The Churches Conservation Trust.

25. Milland, Tuxlith Chapel

Tucked behind the Victorian church of St Luke is a hidden gem, its rustic predecessor
known as Tuxlith Chapel. The documented history of the chapel is scarce but it served
an isolated community in the parish of Trotton for 800 years before becoming a
parish church. Sadly, after such a long wait it only enjoyed parochial status for twenty
years before being supplanted by its newly built neighbour. Documentary evidence
may be scarce but architecturally we can see that it is of Norman origin as there is a
blocked-up window of that period in the south wall. It is clear that the earliest work

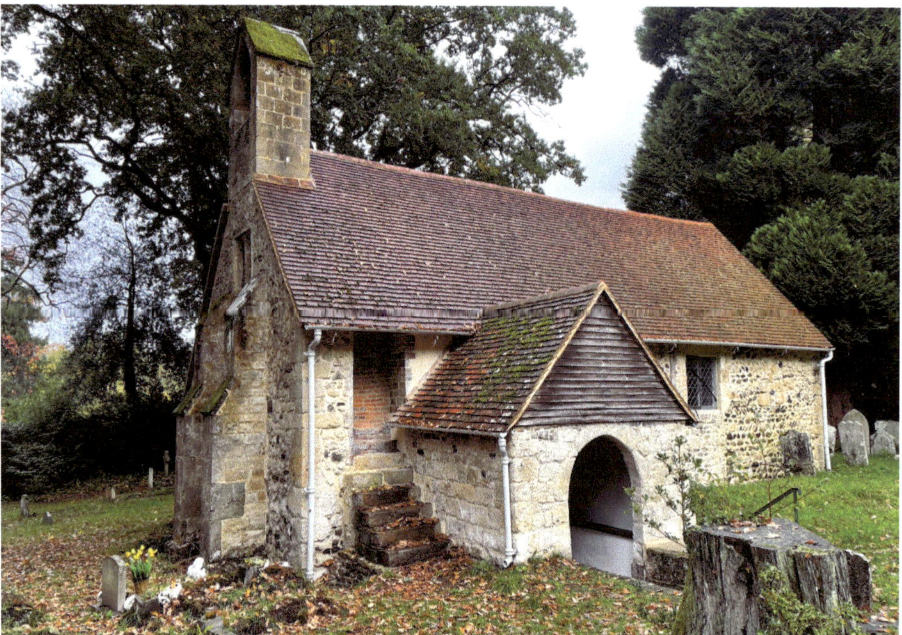

Milland, Tuxlith Chapel. A Norman building that was replaced by a larger church in the
nineteenth century. The steps originally led to an internal west gallery.

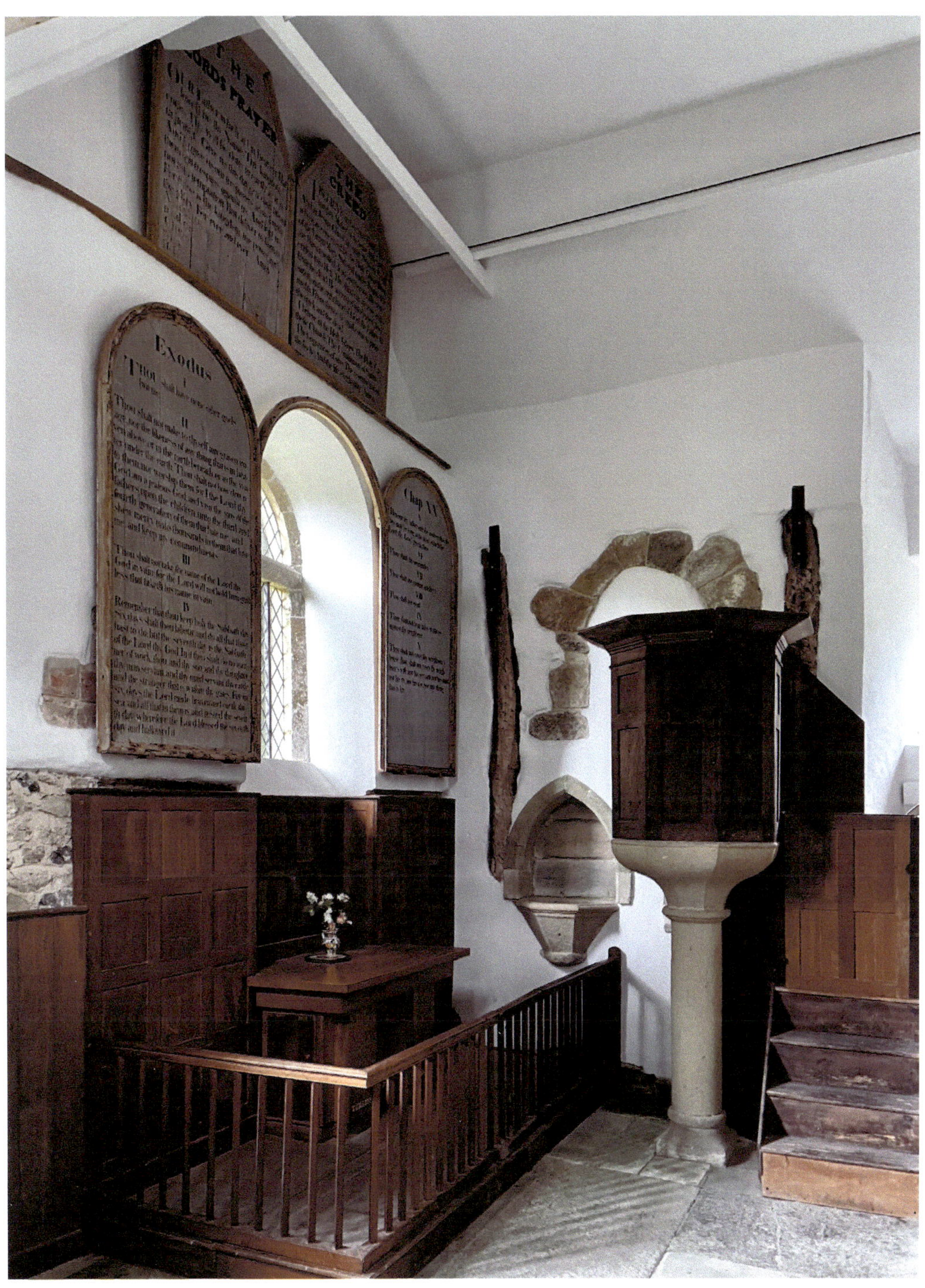

Milland, Tuxlith Chapel. Eighteenth-century commandment boards hang on the east wall as was required by law at the time. Behind the pulpit is a blocked twelfth-century window.

is in ironstone rubble, some of it set in characteristic herringbone form for strength, whilst later alterations used stone from a different source. Next to the south porch is a stone staircase which formerly led to a gallery at the west end. Having its own staircase meant that the poor, for whom the gallery had been constructed, wouldn't have to use the same door as those inhabiting the rented pews in the nave. Stepping inside we find that the interior is mostly empty. After the congregation moved next door, the building was neglected and eventually fell into complete ruin. It was saved by The Friends of Friendless Churches, a national charity, helped by a group of local enthusiasts. It is possible to see where the west gallery ran, and the remnants of a west tower revealed in the masonry of the west wall. In the nineteenth century a north transept was added, also with a gallery, where once again the upper doorway can still be seen. They really were 'packing them in', so it is obvious why they needed a larger building. All is light in the chapel with clear glass which allows the visitor to appreciate the surviving eighteenth-century fittings. The east wall displays the Decalogue, Lord's Prayer and Creed over the small Holy Table set within plain rails. The table itself was designed by Sir Hubert Bennett (d. 2000). Yet these furnishings are partly hidden by the tall eighteenth-century pulpit on a stone wineglass stem that also incorporates the reading desk – a true two-decker. It would have given the parson excellent views into the tall box pews and galleries and shows that here the spoken word was of greater importance to Georgian churchgoers than Holy Communion.

26. Mountfield, All Saints

Standing high on a prominent ridge, this small church has much to draw the visitor. First have a look at the outside of the north nave wall. It is a perfect example of 'vertical archaeology' where many alterations can be found in the stonework. There is a prominent blocked north door and two Norman windows. In the fourteenth century these were filled in and replaced by a much larger window between the two which, in turn, was removed by the Victorians who returned the wall to its original configuration. The church is entered though a charming fourteenth-century wooden porch of cruck construction. It may look venerable but in fact the wood was so decayed that in the early nineteenth century the crucks were turned around, and you can see the much-weathered surface on the inner face. There are seats in the porch for those witnessing the secular legal transactions that formerly took place there and the eagle eyed may spot some double V graffiti which was a familiar medieval apotropaic mark calling on the protection of Our Lady. The chancel arch dates from the original Norman church, whilst to either side of it are thirteenth-century hagioscopes which allowed priests at side altars to coordinate their Mass with the priest at the main altar in the chancel. Above is a wall covered by medieval paintings. The earliest designs are thirteenth century and take the form of brick-like red lines. Slightly later these were overlain by the IHS Sacred Name of Jesus. Following the Reformation, the whole was limewashed over and God-fearing texts painted over the top. Now all three layers are visible together, making it rather difficult to differentiate. Of the most recent paintings it is probably easiest to pick out the injunction 'Thou Shalt Not Steale'. The chancel contains three interesting stained-glass windows. The east window includes a little vignette of the church by Hugh Powell (1972). In the south wall are four Acts of Mercy by Lavers, Barraud and Westlake (1884) whilst the triangular window

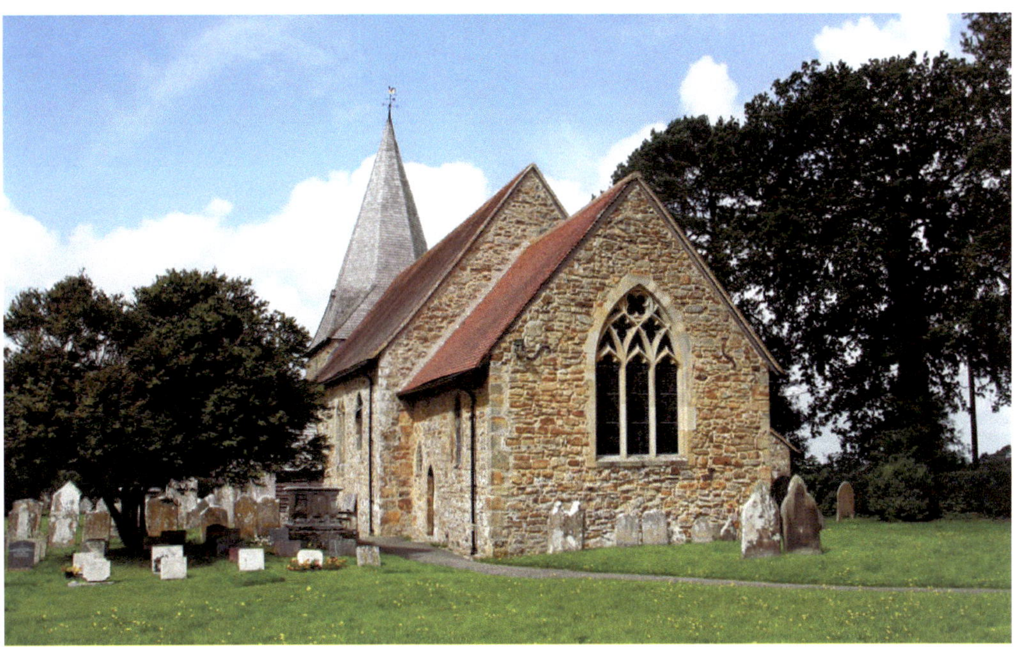

Above: Mountfield. The sandstone churches of East Sussex are in marked contrast to the flint churches to be found in most of the county.

Right: Mountfield. This medieval porch dates from the fourteenth century. Its upright timbers were reversed as they were so weathered, so it now presents its original interior face.

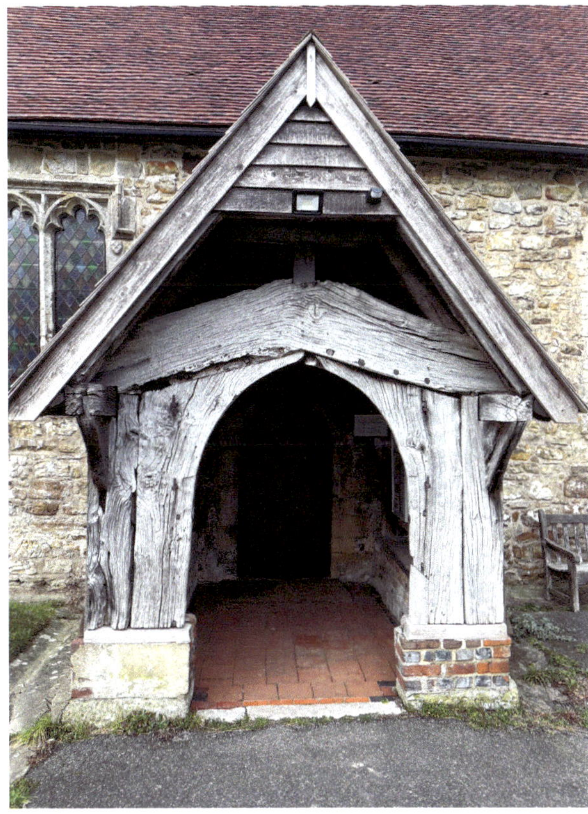

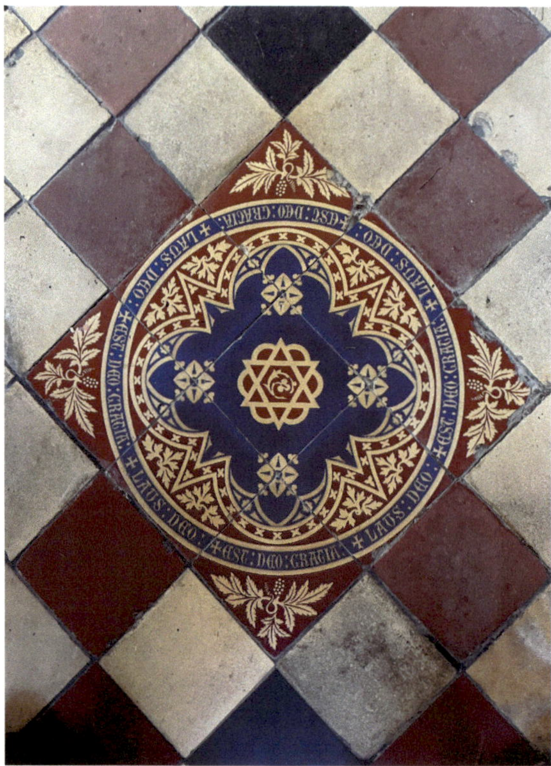

Mountfield. These colourful nineteenth-century tiles were installed as part of the Victorian restoration of the chancel.

depicting the Baptism of Christ is by Martin Travers (1924). Don't miss the lovely nineteenth-century tiles in the centre of the chancel floor which are such a contrast to the surrounding plain tiles.

27. NORTH STOKE, ST MARY THE VIRGIN

Occupying one of the finest settings of any Sussex church, St Mary's may be found on a promontory bounded by a curve of the River Arun and reached by car via a lane running from Amberley station. All medieval churches were dedicated to an individual saint but following the Reformation they were usually known just by the name of the place, and over the course of many generations the original dedication could be forgotten. The Victorians brought many dedications back into use but where records hadn't survived it was often impossible to determine. This was the case here until 2007 when two history students discovered a medieval document in the National Archives which told them that this had been dedicated to St Mary the Virgin. The church has its origins in the early Norman period, with a major enlargement in the thirteenth century when transepts were added. There are several other churches in Sussex which had transepts added to the nave to be used as side chapels for the laity to use. Above the chancel arch are remains of wall paintings, which include a delightful owl – seen in the medieval period as a bird of suspicion and of the dark, rather than the wise creature we think of today. Both transepts have their east windowsills lowered to form a reredos for an altar, and at the junction of nave and chancel are image niches

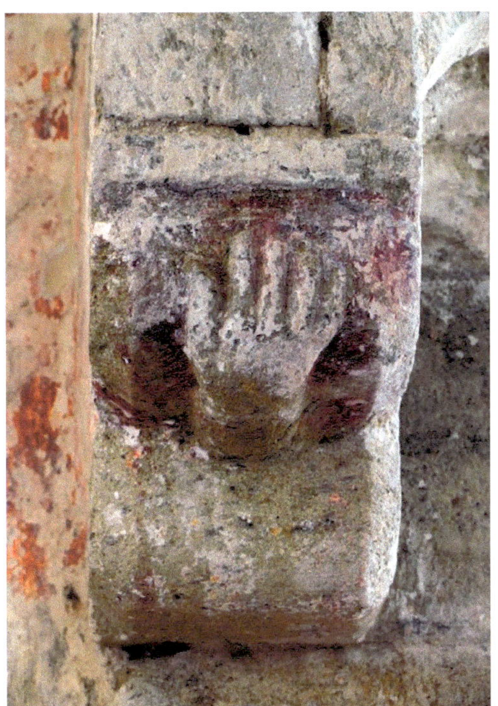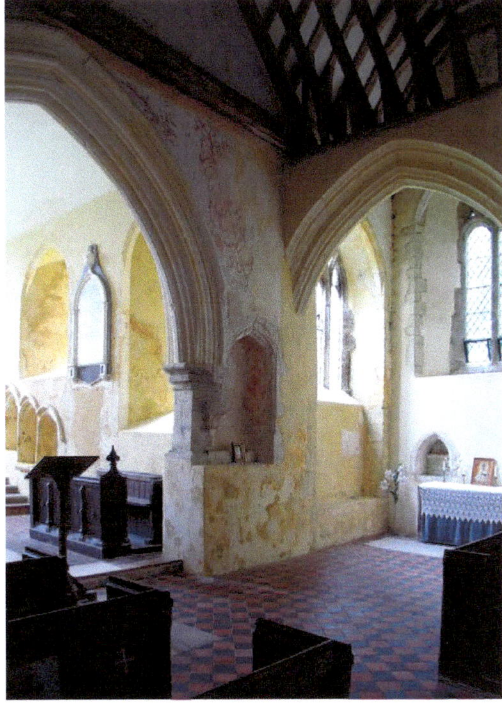

Above left: North Stoke. This small hand was added by a thirteenth-century stonemason to 'hold up' an arch. Traces of its original red paint may be seen.

Above right: North Stoke. The walls are totally unrestored and, in many places, medieval painted designs are peeping through. The arched niche in the centre would have housed a statue. (Image by John Salmon)

to hold images of saints. On the northern side, between the two carved arches, the stonemason has added a little hand, jokingly supporting the stonework above! In the south transept an arched seat has been built into the west wall. This must have been for someone of high status, probably the Lord of the Manor, who at that time would have been making his money from wool, so it is no surprise that between the two arches is the carving of a sheep's head. There are fragments of medieval glass here. In the south transept are two pieces that may have come from an Annunciation scene, whilst in the chancel east window are the better-preserved images of Our Lady and a King. They are composite figures, created using old glass that may not be in the correct positions, but charming, nonetheless. The fact that this church wasn't touched too heavily by the Victorians means that its uneven walls and clear glass create an atmospheric interior that makes a long journey worthwhile.

28. OLD SHOREHAM, ST NICOLAS

Here is a substantial late Saxon building which was enlarged by the Normans and further rebuilt in the fourteenth century. Today the entrance is via the south transept, but a blocked Saxon door in the south wall shows that there was originally access here. As a result, the nave is almost forgotten after the glories of the crossing that you first enter, but it needs to be visited as it contains the treasure of this building – what may be the oldest rood beam in the country. Every church had a rood beam on which stood the figures of the Crucified Christ, Our Lady and St John. When the statues became illegal in the sixteenth century the beams on which they stood were frequently removed as well. Add to that the fact that most were just unadorned pieces of wood and you have a good reason why so many disappeared. Here the beam was carved to match the stone arch below it, which not only helps us date it to the twelfth century but helps prove its importance to the structure. The nearby crossing arches are a delight with much carving – don't miss the cat in the nave and the many different heads elsewhere. Originally there was a Norman chancel and apsidal chapels too, but these were replaced in a series of changes to the east in the fourteenth century. On the exterior north wall of the chancel there is a piscina, indicating that there was once a chapel here, entered from the north transept in its first phase of enlargement. The light chancel is entered via a fourteenth-century screen which seems to have been moved around the building as it doesn't properly fit. To the south is a glazed low side window for ventilating the chancel during Mass whilst nearby is a brass memorial, set within an arch, to Richard Poole who died in 1652. In his thirties he had sailed in the fleet which repelled the 1588 Spanish Armada. The painted ceiling of the chancel dates from the restoration of 1853 when lots of recutting of old stone was undertaken to improve the building and make it even more 'medieval' than it was. Most of the

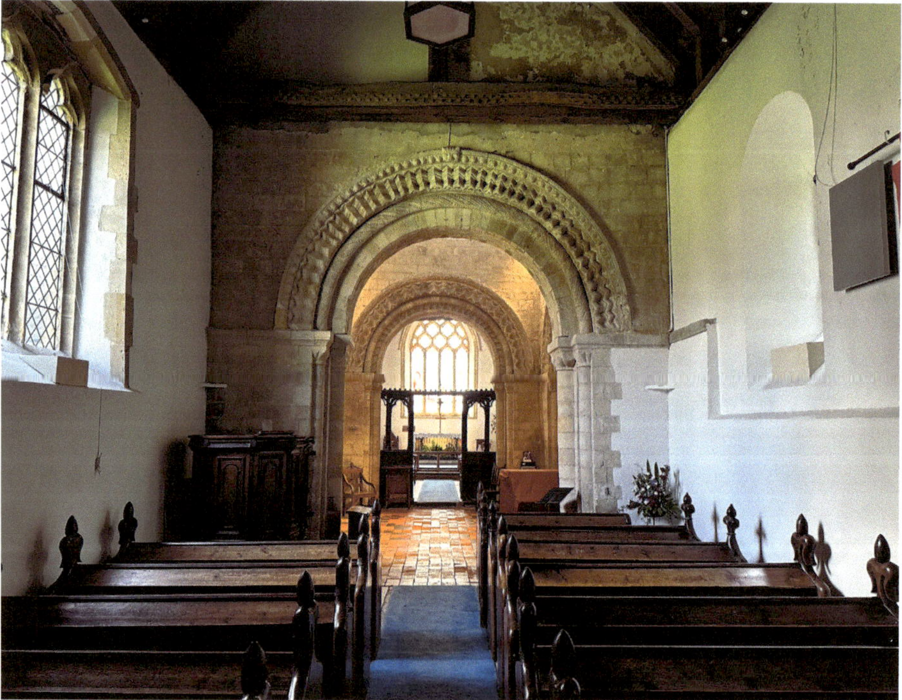

Old Shoreham. Interior looking east through the two Romanesque arches of the crossing tower. The beam above the nearest arch is probably the oldest rood beam to survive the Reformation.

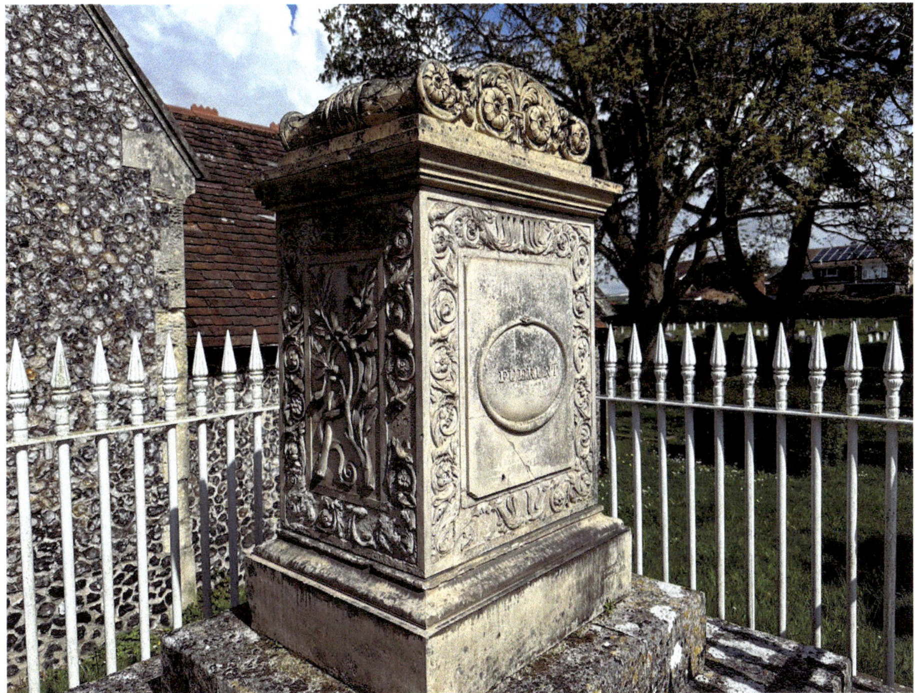

Old Shoreham. On the north side of the church is this impressive monument made of Coade stone, signed Croggan who managed the firm at the time. The only inscription on it is Fuerunt, which means 'I have been'.

stained glass is Victorian including the odd bishop in the south wall whose head doesn't seem to fit. To the north of the church is a huge monument set within white railings. This is made of artificial Coade stone which hardly weathers, and which was popular from the 1780s to 1820s. Usually these are signed Coade, but this is signed Croggan, who was running the firm in 1828 when this was erected. Sadly it does not tell us who it commemorates.

29. Ovingdean, St Wulfran

It would be impossible to imagine a more rural spot, and even more so when you realise how close to Brighton this church is. Built into a valley through the Downs, St Wulfran's is a simple church of tower, nave and chancel with a tiny rebuilt south chapel. Wulfran was a French archbishop in the eighth century who is associated with saving people from drowning. This is a much-loved church built into a sheltered hillside with a huge yew tree protecting the south entrance. The tower is finished with a typical Sussex Cap pyramid. Recycling is nothing new as the step into the church is formed of some poor soul's headstone. Inside there is much of interest as Ovingdean was the birthplace of Charles Eamer Kempe, the most prominent church furnisher of the Victorian era, whose work may be found in 7,000 churches worldwide. Unsurprisingly he left an enormous corpus of work in his home county, but more especially here in the village of his birth. There is stained glass by him, a prominent

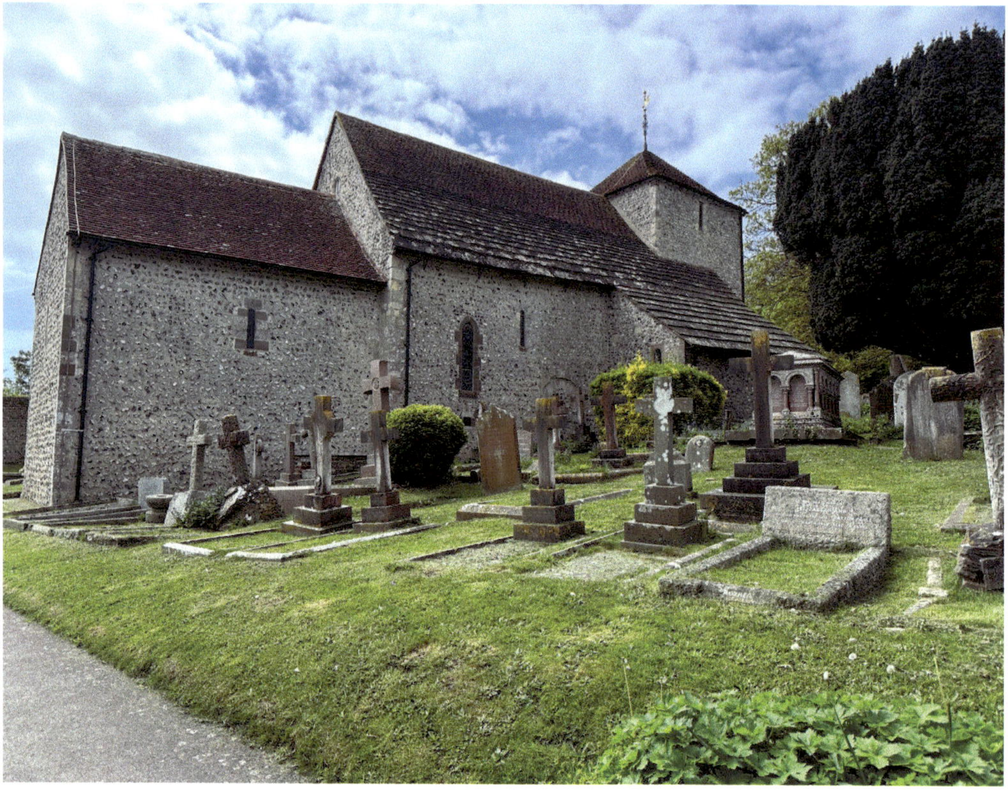

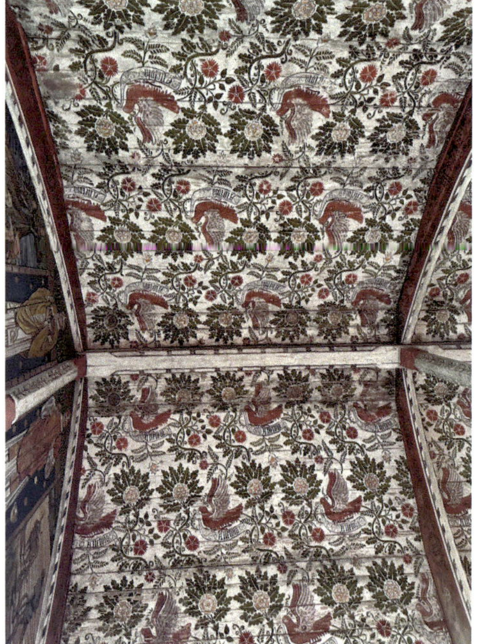

Above: Ovingdean. Exterior from the north showing how the church is built against the hillside. The two small windows are Norman, the larger one thirteenth century. The tower has a typical 'Sussex Cap' roof.

Left: Ovingdean. This painted ceiling was designed by Charles Eamer Kempe in 1865 and was one of many contributions he made to the church in the village of his birth.

rood with a celure or canopy above the chancel arch, his own funeral hatchment high on the south wall and, most impressive of them all, the painted ceiling of the chancel which has been recently cleaned. Kempe's stained glass has a style that is easy to recognise (although it was frequently copied – see the entry for Streat). He started making glass in the 1860s and from the 1890s he often signed his glass with a wheatsheaf from his shield of arms, and this continued (with an added tower) after his death in 1907 until the closure of the firm in 1934. The central chancel arch is Norman, but the arches either side are not. In the south wall of the chancel is a door leading into a tiny south chapel, but as you can see by the Norman window to the right of it, this chapel was a slightly later addition. To the right of the door is a low side window which dates from the thirteenth century, which goes to show that it was an outside wall by that time. The churchyard contains the grave of Kempe, opposite the door, whilst nearby is that of Magnus Volk, inventor of the electric railway which still runs along Brighton seafront.

30. PARHAM, ST PETER

A church in the park of the 'big house' and through its monuments telling the story of the estate and its owners. At one stage it was probably a typical Norman church of two cells, but various additions and alterations have made it a difficult building to decipher. It's not helped by the fact that the north side, facing the mansion, is covered with 'Roman cement', which not only makes the building forbidding, but also hides any clues the walls there might be able to give us. By contrast the south side is a delight with Horsham slab roof, gothick windows, an almost separate south chapel and a toybox tower. We have documentary evidence that the south chapel was built in 1545 and today it contains a number of simple memorial tablets to eighteenth- and nineteenth-century owners of the estate. Whilst the tower is medieval, its present appearance is of the late Georgian period when a huge amount of work was carried out by Sir Cecil Bishop. He more or less rebuilt the nave and chancel in gothick form (using the pointed arch as decoration, rather than structure). His are the nave windows and the plaster ceilings. That in the chancel is rather peculiar with little plaster decorations that remind me of an elephant's trunk. He filled the nave with box pews focussed on the two-decker pulpit. Opposite the pulpit is a small transept built for the Manorial Pew. It has its own entrance so that m'Lord didn't have to mix with his tenants and it has additional comfort in the form of a fireplace. The family could sit here and follow the service without being watched by the rest of the congregation. If they wanted to make their presence known they only needed to stoke the fire! So here we have a typically late Georgian interior. However, there is one unexpected feature that makes this church unique. It has the most important lead font in the country which dates from the fourteenth century. Furthermore, it can be dated through its heraldry to 1351. It carries a repeated pattern of an heraldic shield and an inscription in Lombardic characters which reads *Jesus of Nazareth*. Other lead fonts survive nearby at Edburton and Poynings but this takes pride of place and is of museum quality. You may wonder who attended this church as it lost its village in the late eighteenth century when the landscape was 'improved' and now enjoys its splendid isolation.

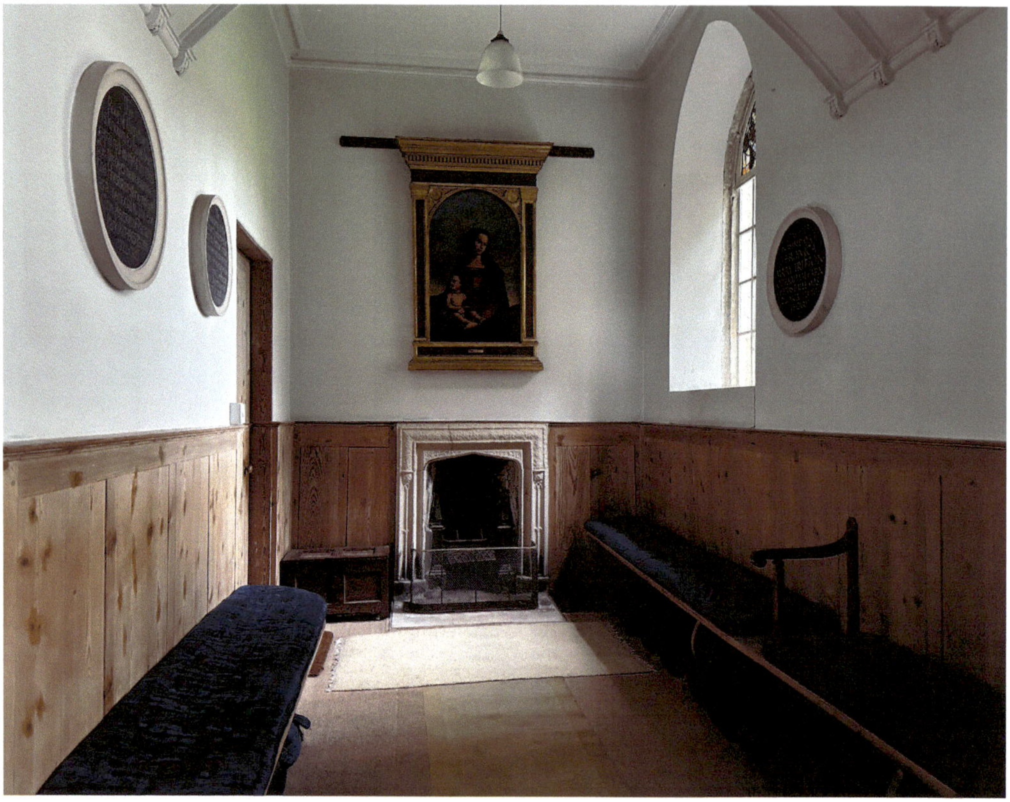

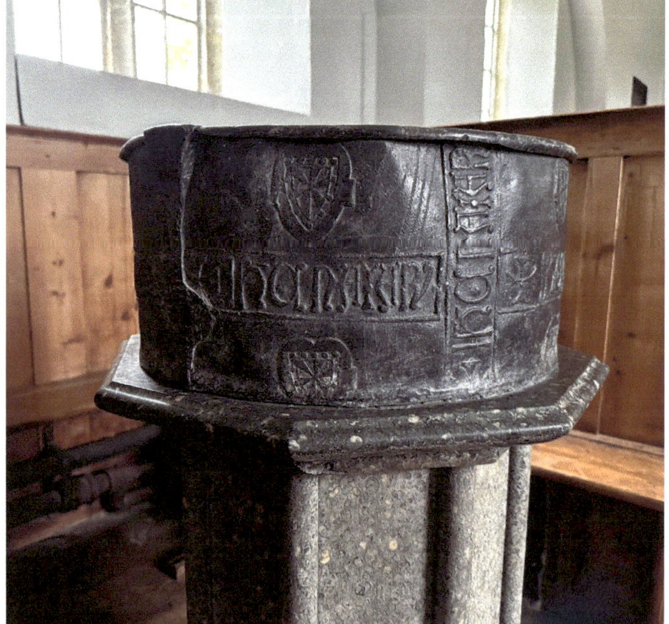

Above: Parham. The Lords of the Manor sat in splendid isolation in the north transept of the church, warmed by an open fire and entered by a private door.

Left. Parham. The lead font dates from the fourteenth century and can be dated by its heraldry to 1351. It bears the repeated Latin inscription 'Jesus of Nazareth'.

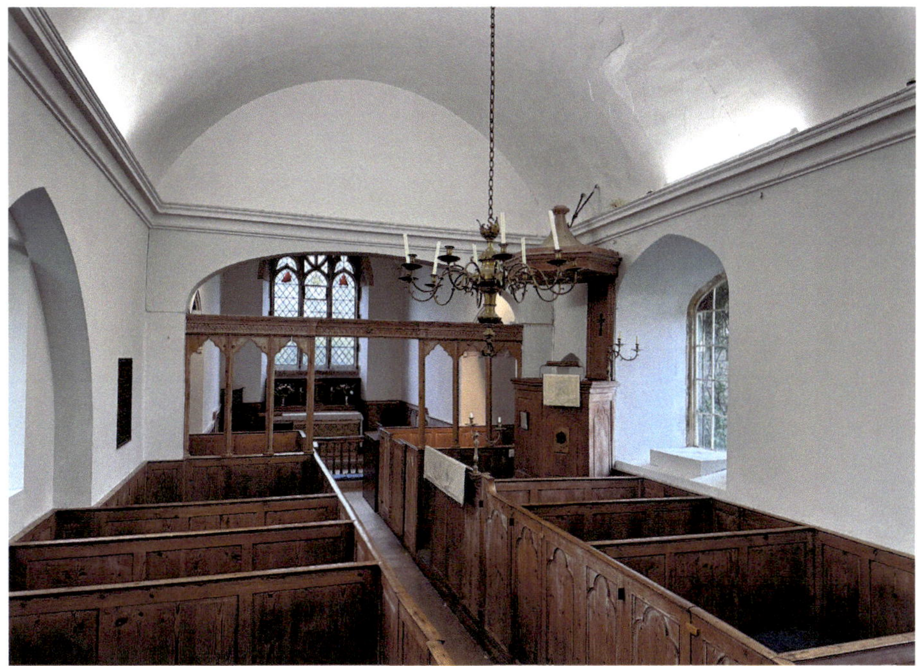

Parham. The nave is filled with box pews, each of which had a good view of the pulpit which was at the heart of the Georgian service. The ceiling helped prevent draughts and kept the church clean.

31. PENHURST, ST MICHAEL

One of the most remote churches in Sussex, and well worth the circuitous journey to find it. Small and well cared for, what it lacks in architectural pretension it more than makes up for in often-missed details. Consisting of fifteenth-century tower, nave and chancel with a seventeenth-century north chapel now used as a meeting room, it is one of the smallest churches in the area and must have seemed rather full in March 1851 when the Census of Religious Worship recorded fifty-three attendees at afternoon service. The nave is filled with box pews with very low doors which are dated 1858. The pulpit and desk are of seventeenth-century date and are reputed to have come from another church, although this part of Sussex was known for similar woodwork at the time. The font stands at the east end of the nave, rather than at its more usual location near the west end, and behind it is a hagioscope which tells us that its position was originally taken by a side altar. The hagioscope allowed a priest at this nave altar to see his colleague at the main altar. The rood screen itself is contemporary with the building of the church, although it has lost its loft. We call it the rood screen because it stood beneath the rood – the figure of the Crucified Christ which all medieval churches would have displayed. This was destroyed at the Reformation but we can see where it would have hung on the front of the easternmost kingpost of the roof, and those with good eyesight (or binoculars) will see that the hook which supported it is still there. This is a terribly rare survivor. Under the tower, which was never completed, and now set into the wall, is a rare setting-out stone which assisted masons

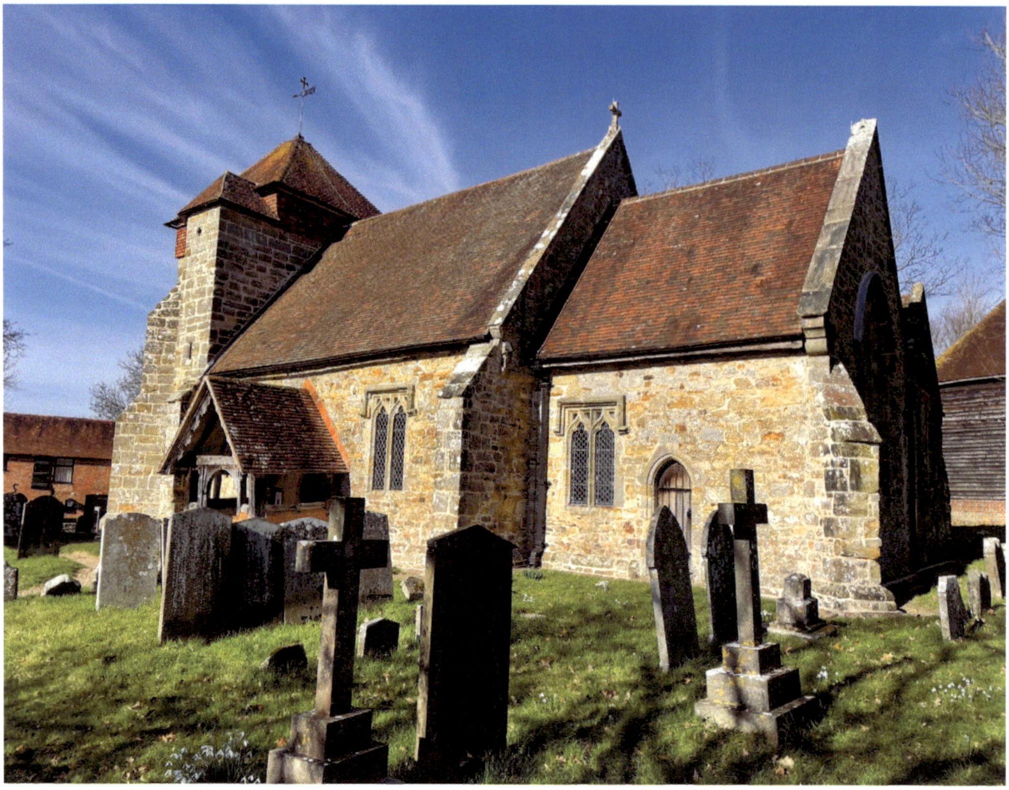

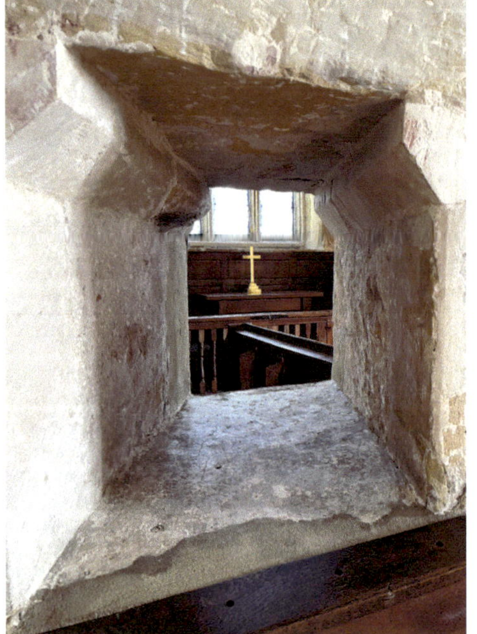

Above: Penhurst. The isolated church is built on a knoll and is unusual in possessing nothing earlier than the fourteenth century.

Left: Penhurst. A view through the hagioscope to the High Altar would have allowed a priest serving at an altar in the nave, with his back to the congregation, to see his fellow priest.

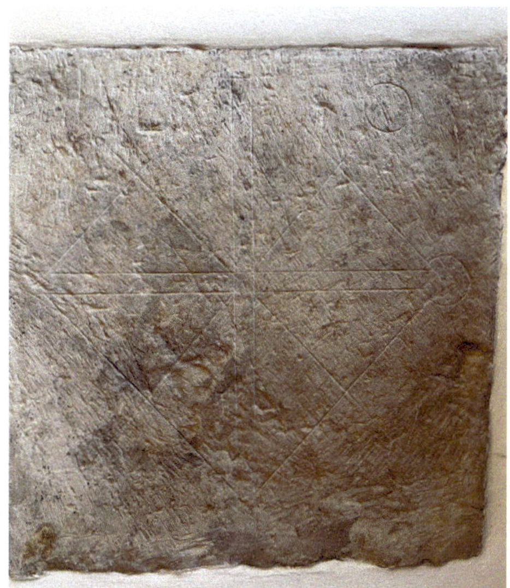

Penhurst. This slab was a setting-out stone which, in effect, was a template for stonemasons to make sure their work was of a standard size and shape, using exact angles.

to keep their mouldings a standard size and shape. Occasionally found in cathedrals, it is rare to find one in a parish church. The actor Harry H. Corbett (d. 1982), best known for his role as Harold Steptoe, is buried in the churchyard extension.

32. POLING, ST NICHOLAS

Reached by a long footpath at the edge of the village, this is a building of great charm. The nave is pre-Conquest and contains one double-splayed window indicating this early date. But what makes this window unique is that preserved inside a display case are pieces of the original wooden shutter that closed it. Glass didn't become widespread in country churches until the thirteenth century and prior to that the openings were shuttered in windy weather. These pieces only survived because the window was walled up when it was no longer required and the shutter was walled up within it. Dividing nave and chancel is a low wooden screen, the south section of which is medieval and has three openings cut into it. These would have allowed someone kneeling in the nave to have had a view of the main altar. In the centre of the chancel is a late fifteenth-century memorial brass to Walter Davy, priest of the church. The upper doorway of the rood loft survives but the present rood beam doesn't belong here and is at too low a level. In the twentieth century much art was brought into the church. The reredos is of painted panels and incorporates the patron saint, St Nicholas. No longer on the font, but by the altar, is a seventeenth-century-style font cover with similarly painted panels. A more recent artwork is the altar frontal depicting St Nicholas with a tree in different seasons behind him – St Nicholas not just being around at Christmas! As you leave there is a wooden pillar donations box, the metalwork of which carries the date 1797. Secured in the porch is the gravestone of Alice Woolldridge who died in 1740 and which carries the rhyme: *The world is a round thing, and full of crooked streets. Death is a market Place where all men meet. If life was a thing that money could buy, the rich would live and the poor would dye.* In the churchyard you can find the grave of cricketer Colin Cowdray.

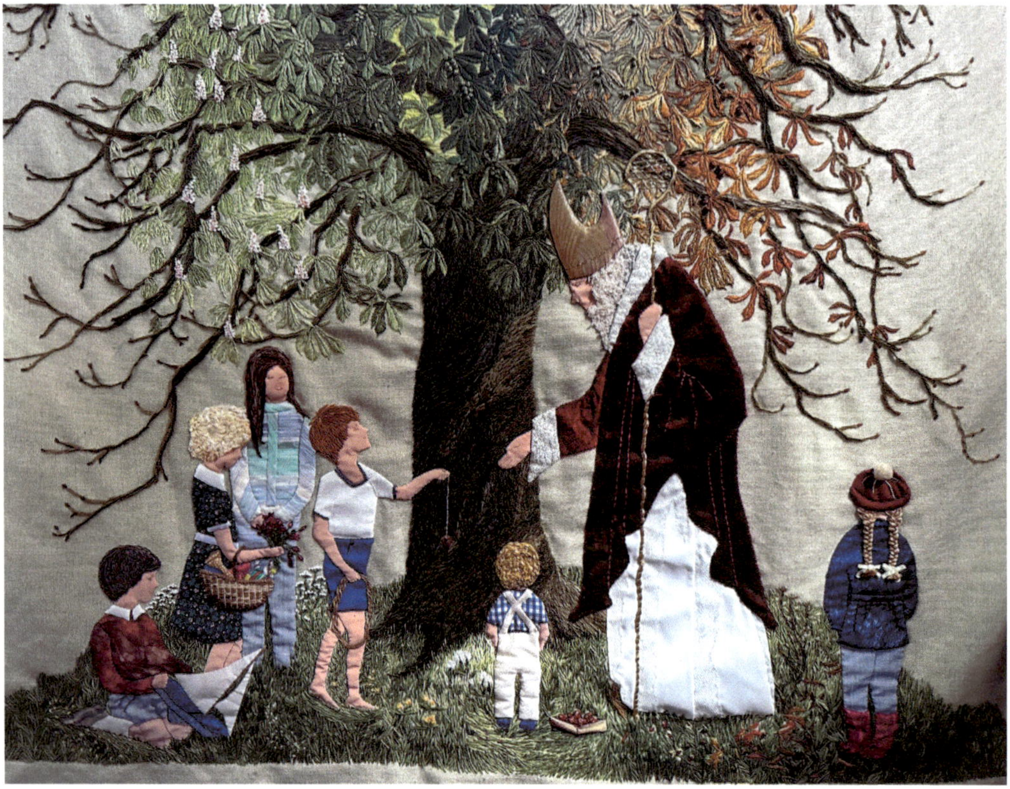

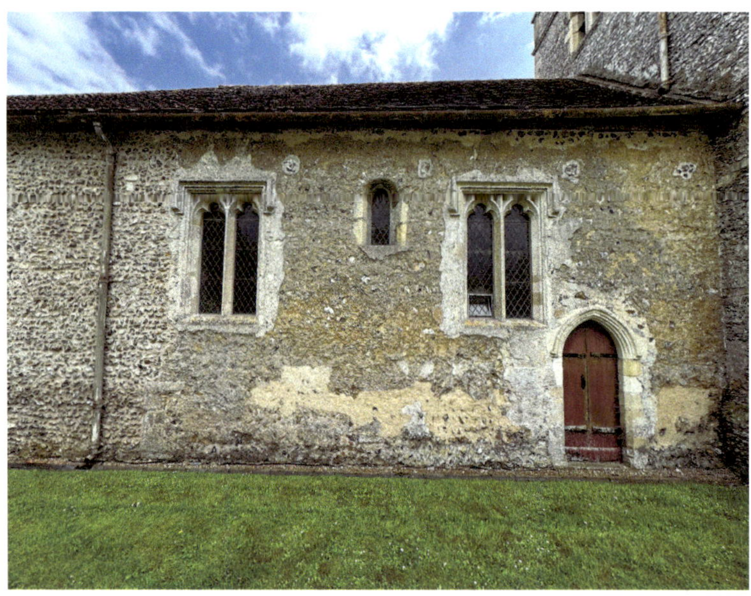

Poling. The patron saint of the church is St Nicholas and this frontal by Jill Adams depicts him throughout the year, and not just at Christmas. All seasons are depicted in the tree behind.

Poling. The north wall of the nave shows an original double-splayed Saxon window in the centre as well as the two larger fourteenth-century windows which replaced it.

33. POYNINGS, HOLY TRINITY

One of a series of churches that run along the north side of the South Downs and which are all worthy of study. What makes this stand out is that it was built in one go in the mid-fourteenth century, at a time when many earlier churches were being remodelled. It was constructed by Lord Poynings (d. 1369) who left a bequest in his will towards its construction. It is a textbook example of a church built on a cruciform plan, with transepts designed to be chapels. Because of its date it is architecturally on the cusp of the Decorated and Perpendicular styles, which makes its window tracery quite unusual. Ignore the south transept window, which was a replacement, but all the others are contemporary with the building. When originally filled with painted glass these must have brought people from far and wide to marvel at it as no other local church could boast of architecture this impressive. Sadly just a few random pieces of original glass remain. Externally, the walls are built of local flint which has been knapped to reveal its shiny inside, whilst the corners of the building are of sandstone. Every so often the flints reveal patterns of three sandstone blocks. These are infilled putlog holes, where the scaffolding had been built into the walls as they went up. When the wall was dry the scaffolding was removed and the holes filled with flint. In the event of the wall needing repair, it would be easy to scrape

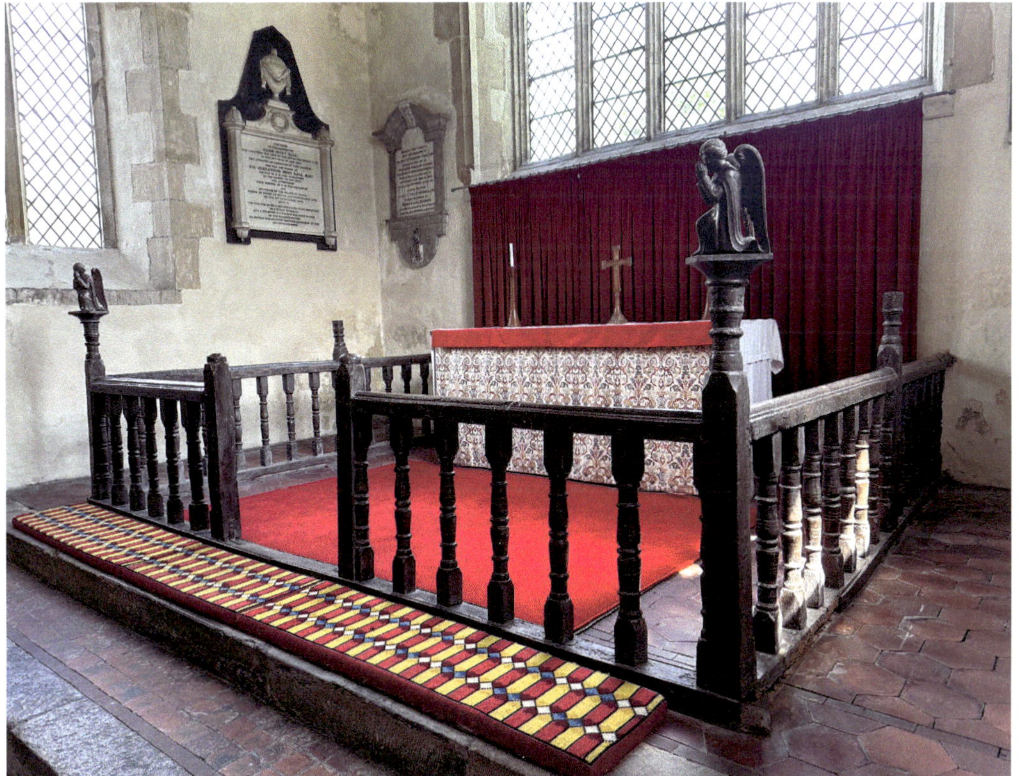

Poynings. The altar rails are known as 'Laudian style' and were introduced to recreate a sacred space that had been lost at the Reformation. The two angels are not original.

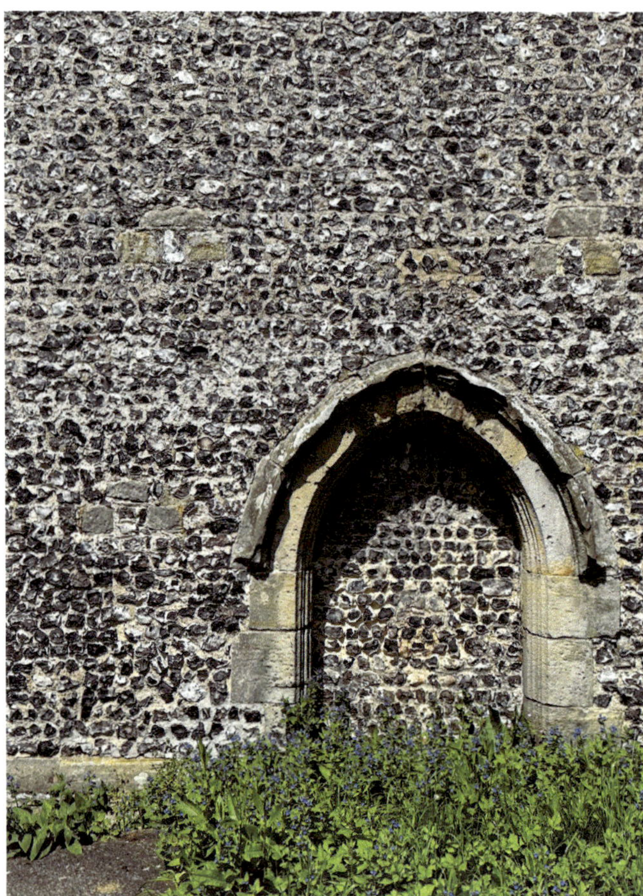

Poynings. It is possible to see here the three putlog holes that held the scaffolding poles as the wall was built. They are edged with dressed stone and were filled with flint as the scaffolding was taken down.

out these infilled holes and reinsert scaffolding timbers. Every church had them but they are more visible here because of the visual difference between knapped flints and sandstone blocks. Inside, all the dressed stone is sandstone which creates a solid effect. By the door is the fourteenth-century font which, unusually, does not have a separate base but is constructed as a single entity with blank arcading. The north transept is now the vestry but you can see medieval memorials on the floor. The south transept still fulfils its function as a chapel and is entered through a wooden screen. The floor has many stone coffin lids, some dating from before the construction of the church, so they must have been in the earlier building. The best preserved is under the altar, where you will also see excellent-quality medieval tiles collected from other parts of the church. The pulpit is a good example of local work of the seventeenth century with deeply incised decoration whilst the chancel contains Laudian altar rails, which surround the Holy Table on three sides and were preferred by the seventeenth-century Archbishop William Laud as they created a 'sacred space' which prevented the communion table being moved about the church and being used for other, possibly secular, things. Once a common feature of our churches, they often disappeared during Victorian restorations when the east end of our chancels were reordered.

34. PRESTON PARK, ST PETER

St Peter's is one of the county's retired churches and stands next to Preston Manor, which is now a museum. It lays claim to being the oldest standing building in Brighton and Hove, dating from around 1200. The architecture of the church shows that it once served a large and wealthy parish of sheep farmers whose wealth was short-lived and which had disappeared by the time of the fourteenth-century Black Death. Little happened here until the nineteenth century when the church was restored and the twentieth century when it had a major fire. The porch roof is of Horsham slab, which must once have covered the whole building, otherwise the exterior has a mechanical Victorian feel to it. Inside, the most famous aspect of the furnishings are the wall paintings. One shows the martyrdom of St Thomas Becket and dates from the early thirteenth century – possibly painted by someone who had been alive at the time of Becket's death. Nearby is a very faded Nativity scene, whilst on the south side of the chancel arch is an excellent depiction of St Michael weighing souls with Our Lady interceding to save just one. The chancel was beautified by the Stanford family in the late Victorian era with high-quality mosaic floors and later stencilled walls which have recently been cleaned. Interestingly, the carved stone altar is a reused table tomb that originally stood against the north wall. It depicts the shields of arms of the

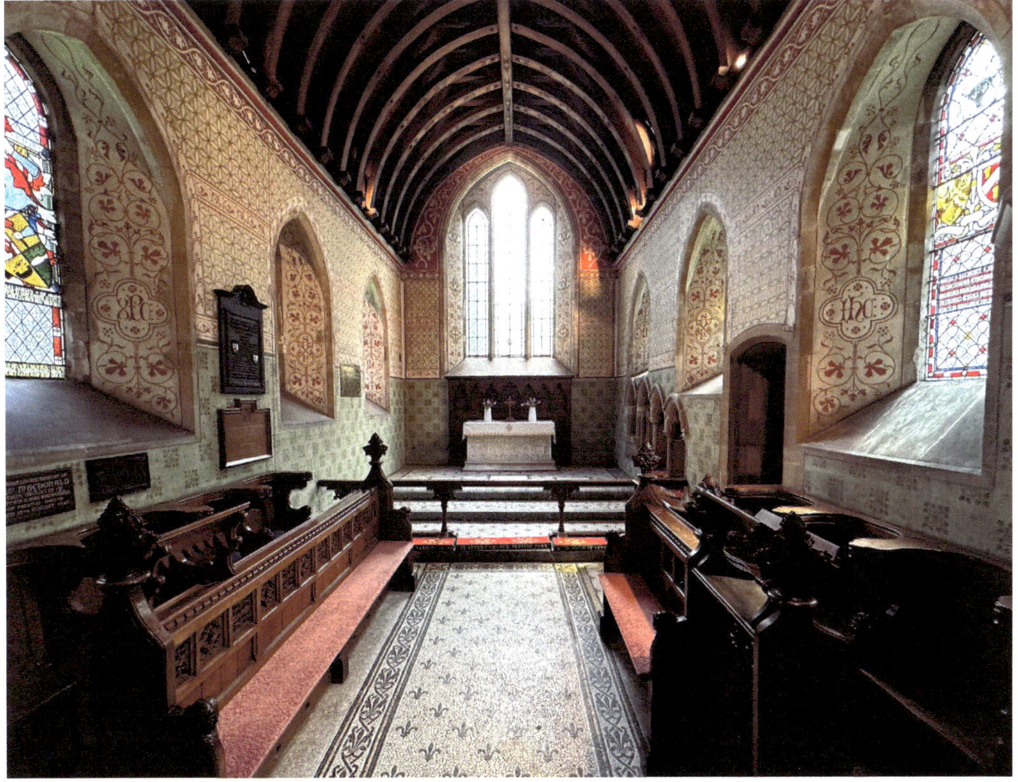

Preston Park, St Peter. Interior of the chancel with stencilled decoration from the Edwardian era. The altar formerly stood against the north wall and was built as the Elrington tomb.

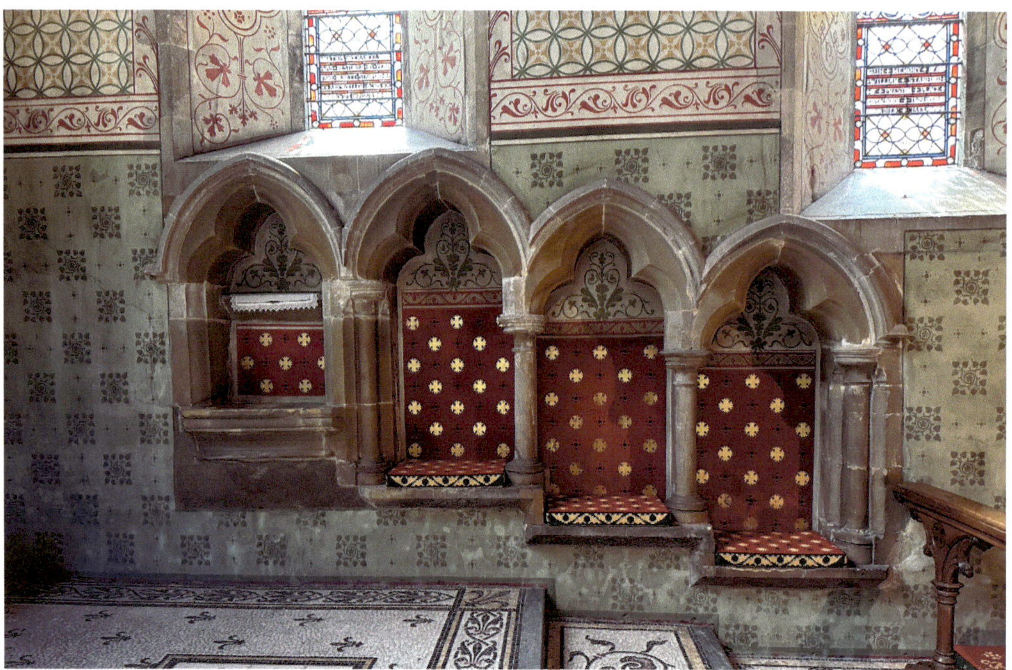

Preston Park. The thirteenth-century sedilia for priest, deacon and sub-deacon can no longer be used as the floor level has been raised. On the left is the piscina where the priest washed the sacred vessels after Mass.

various families to whom Edward Elrington (d. 1515) was related. He was a tenant of the manor next door. When new it must have been brightly painted. Nearby is a stained-glass window by a local firm, Barton, Kinder and Alderson, depicting the Good Samaritan. Their studios were in Prestonville Road behind Brighton station. By the door is a tablet commemorating Isaac Gold (d. 1861), a businessman who was murdered on the train as he travelled home to Preston Park from London. The police published an image of their suspect for the first time to help them in his arrest and conviction.

35. PYECOMBE, CHURCH OF THE TRANSFIGURATION

This little church has stood on its prominent knoll for over 800 years, but since the bypass was built its location has been somewhat marred by the sound of traffic on the A23. You enter the churchyard through a fine example of a Tapsel Gate. These are a Sussex speciality and are designed so that the whole gate pivots on a central post. One tradition says that they were designed this way so that a coffin could be stood on them at the start of the funeral service, but that would be impossible here as the handle takes the form of a shepherd's crook and protrudes. From the north the church looks rather dark and unpromising; only the tower's little Sussex Cap relieves the scene. But once inside we discover a gem of an interior. The chancel arch is the original, although when you look at it closely the original stones have been recut. The two openings, one each side, are not Norman and were probably cut through

Right: Pyecombe. This thirteenth-century lead font probably escaped destruction during the Commonwealth period by being plastered over. Remains of the plaster can still be seen.

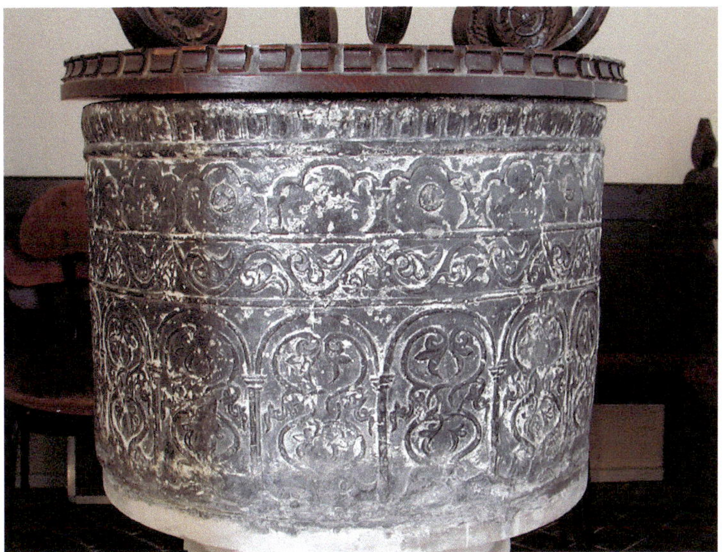

Below: Pyecombe. The entrance to the churchyard is formed by a 'Tapsel Gate' which pivots on its central post and which is a Sussex speciality.

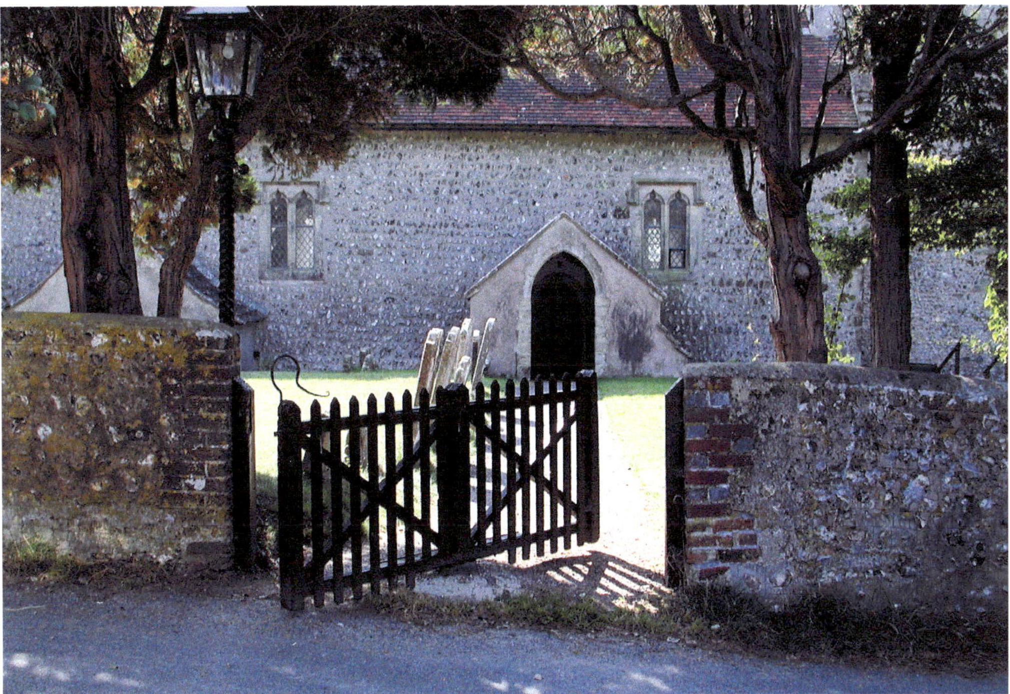

after the Reformation to make the chancel more accessible, as can also be found at Ovingdean. The stonework of the east window is nineteenth century and the glass by Arthur Orr, whose studio was at Harrow and who designed all the stained glass in the church over a twenty-year period. Above the chancel arch hang the royal arms of George III flanked by the Creed, Lord's Prayer and Decalogue. The arms are signed along the bottom by the artist, W. Hamper, and dated 1765. Curiously the artist has also added his age – fifteen. Perhaps it was his idea to provide the lion and unicorn with such piercing eyes! At the west end of the church is a rare lead font. These were once relatively common but many were destroyed during the Wars of the Three Kingdoms (1639–53) when they were melted down for ammunition. This example dates from the thirteenth century and was possibly missed because it had been painted to look like stone. There are only two other lead fonts surviving in the county, at Edburton and Parham. Visitor facilities have recently been added to the church.

36. Rotherfield, St Denys

Built on a majestic scale, the church tells the familiar story of medieval enlargement over a period of centuries. You step into a dark interior but helpful visitor lighting is at hand. The arcades of each aisle provide a textbook example of thirteenth- and fourteenth-century designs, the earlier defined by the round piers, the latter by octagonal. Our eyes are taken up to the unusual wagon roof and then to the extensive wall paintings above and around the chancel arch. The top scene shows Christ in Majesty, sitting on a rainbow. Below this may have been a Doom or Last Judgement

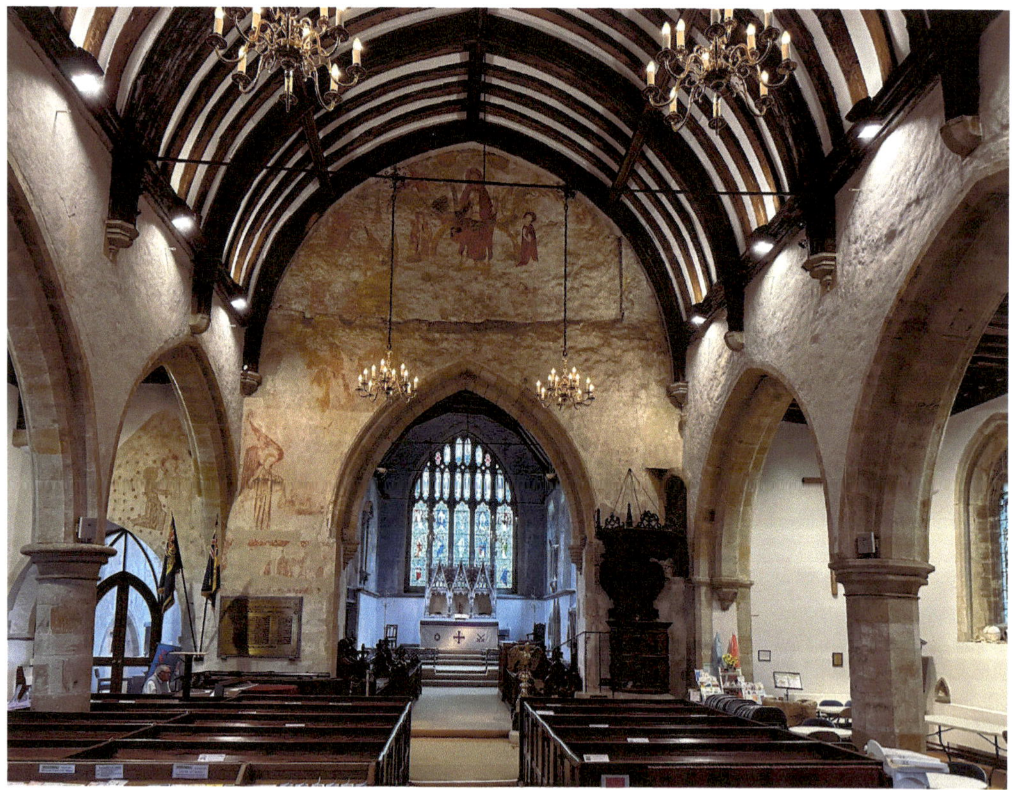

Rotherfield. An exceptionally large church with significant remains of wall paintings. The pulpit is seventeenth century and behind it is the door to the rood loft. The arch of the north arcade dies into the wall, showing that the rood screen ran across the north aisle as well.

scene as on the left-hand side at a lower level we find the image of St Michael holding the scales with which to weigh the souls of the deceased. To the left of this scene, in the north aisle, is an earlier image of the Incredulity of St Thomas, where Christ tells Thomas to touch the wound in his side. It is set off by a background of five-petalled flowers. From here you can enter the north chapel, named after the local Nevill family, patrons of the church, and the oldest structural part visible today. It is incredibly tall and high and on its western wall is a large area of thirteenth-century wall painting depicting cut blocks of stone. The decorative scheme goes around a blocked window, which tells us that the window was there to bring light into the building long before the present north aisle was built. In contrast to the splendour of the rest of the church the chancel is very plain with a simple sedilia and piscina, and a reredos designed by a nineteenth-century member of the Nevill family who was an architect. The church is filled with box pews which rise towards the back. They are probably of early nineteenth-century date and are a rare survivor of that period. The magnificent pulpit is dated 1632 and is an incomer, having been built for the Archbishop of York's palace at Bishopthorpe outside York. It found its way here in the nineteenth century when the Rector of Rotherfield was married to a daughter of Archbishop Thomson. Standing in the south aisle is the true treasure of the church, a sixteenth-century font cover. Now supported on its own stand, it is of the 'enclosed' form (see Ticehurst) and is dated 1533. Whilst the frame represents later remodelling, the panels are original and show the foliate decoration so common at the time and also the heraldry of the Nevill family. Finally, the glass in the east window is by William Morris and dates from 1878.

37. SALEHURST, ST MARY

The church is built of sandstone and stands on a prominent position above the valley of the River Rother. With only a scattering of houses around the church, the main centre of population is at Robertsbridge the other side of the A21. You step under the tower into a barn of a church, mostly dating from the fourteenth century, although there are a few earlier features. Though it is a wide church it is a light one due to the clerestory windows with rere-arches that make the nave brighter than the aisles. Most of these were added in the nineteenth century. In the east wall of the nave are two high windows which originally gave some illumination to the rood, which must have been some way higher than the rood loft judging by the surviving upper doorway to the north of the chancel arch. At the back of the church are four hatchments, my favourite being the one with red and gold quarterings and a green dragon for a member of the Pakenham family. Hidden behind the organ is a fantastic fourteenth-century tomb recess with lavish pinnacles either side which, even in its damaged state, is one of the finest in the county. If you peer even further into the chapel you'll see a thirteenth-century piscina that served an altar here. In the south aisle is the remains of another important memorial set beneath a window, with space for heraldic arms which would once have carried the painted shields of arms of those commemorated, but now the paint has worn off we have no idea who was buried there. A later and more poignant memorial nearby is to Henry Osborne, who was killed at the Battle of Loos in 1915, which was erected by his employers, the Kent and East Sussex Railway. In the same aisle is a millennium window by Alan

Wright containing a verse by Abraham Lincoln. Another fine window is that in the Lady Chapel, designed by Charles Eamer Kempe, with delicate representations of Faith, Hope and Charity. Easily missed at the back of the church are the remains of four tracery lights containing stained glass of birds, dating from the fourteenth century, their brush strokes as clear as the day they were painted. As part of the nineteenth-century restoration many memorials were removed and placed in the western vestries. There are a handful of cast-iron ledger slabs in the floor and many high-quality mural tablets, the most interesting being that to Jane Micklethewaite (d. 1819). It is signed by the sculptor Peter Rouw the younger, a fashionable London sculptor who was also 'modeller to His Majesty'. It depicts a sepulchral urn below which is an open urn surrounded by an ouroboros, a serpent eating its own tail, which is a symbol of eternity. Jane's husband is helpfully described as 'Lay Rector of Salehurst', which tells us that he was responsible for the maintenance of the chancel, which in turn shows that this monument must originally have been in that part of the church.

38. SINGLETON, ST JOHN THE EVANGELIST

Many visitors to the Weald and Downland Museum probably never get to visit the peaceful village of Singleton and this wonderfully atmospheric church. From the outside it is obvious that the tower is Saxon with an early double-splayed window on the north side by the porch. It is a shame that the tower is rendered as it would be interesting to see its various periods of construction. On the south side of the church much character is given by the catslide roof which covers the nave and south aisle. When we find this feature, it often suggests that any Victorian restoration was minimal as they didn't approve of features they saw as dishonest architecture, of which the catslide roof was one. They felt that each compartment of a church required a separate roof. When you step down into the building it is obvious that only essential repairs were carried out by the Victorians as the floor is uneven and the space full of fifteenth-century benches. The nave arcades are thirteenth century, of the familiar circular piers with plain mouldings. The chancel arch is part of the same scheme and it should be noticed that there is no change in floor level between nave and chancel. At the junction is a prominent rood loft staircase where its lower and upper stairs are literally one above the other. The stairs are lit by a tiny window which is visible in the angular filling of the wall outside. The chancel contains two sixteenth-century monuments of Petworth marble. Each takes the form of a stone chest with a backplate and cresting and originally had brasses inset into the stone. The brasses have long disappeared but it is likely that they were fictive tombs for the 12th and 13th Earls of Arundel who held estates here and who are actually buried with the rest of their family at Arundel. It is a shame that the altar rails were crudely set into both of them. To the left of the northern monument is a single bracket in the wall, above the panelling. This shows us where a beam carried the lentern veil across the chancel. During Lent the altar would have been veiled from view by a curtain suspended from this beam. Before you leave, don't miss the graffiti on the chancel arch where seventeenth-century families had fun with their knives, or the delightful medieval hinges on the inside of the north door.

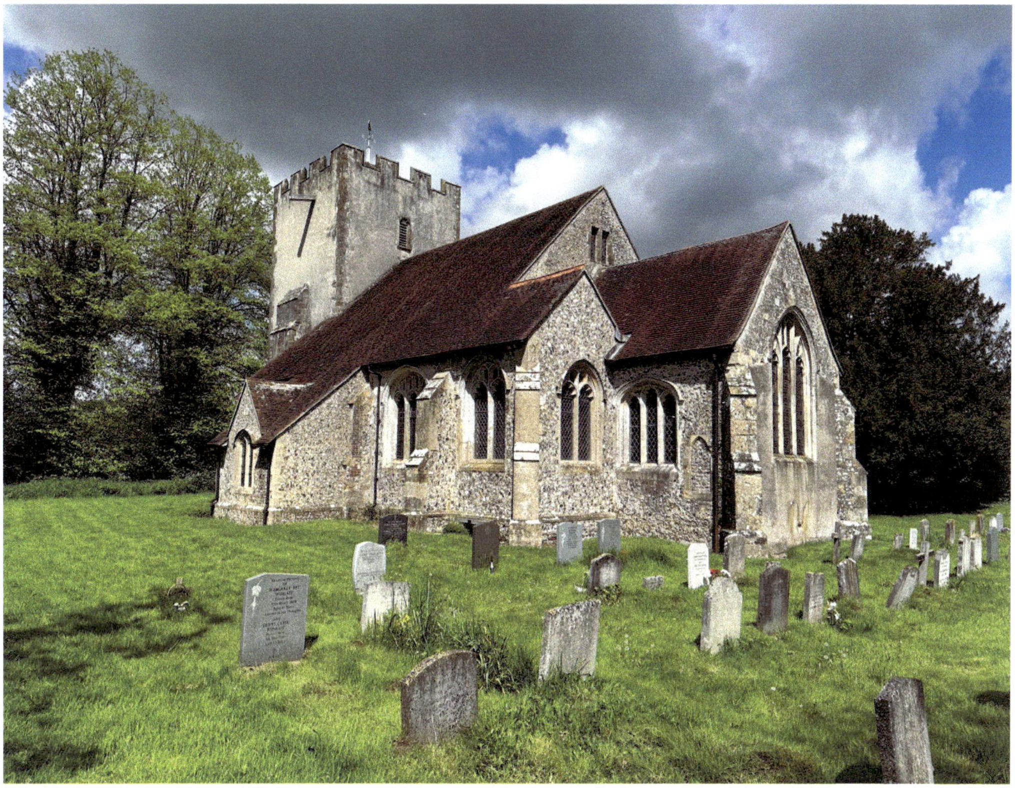

Above: Singleton. Exterior from the southeast showing the complex roof structures of nave, chancel, south aisle and south chapel.

Right: Singleton. Interior looking west shows the doorway opening high in the west wall which would have been the opening to a gallery in Saxon times. The extreme height of the walls is a good indicator of a Saxon structure, even though the current arcades date from the thirteenth century.

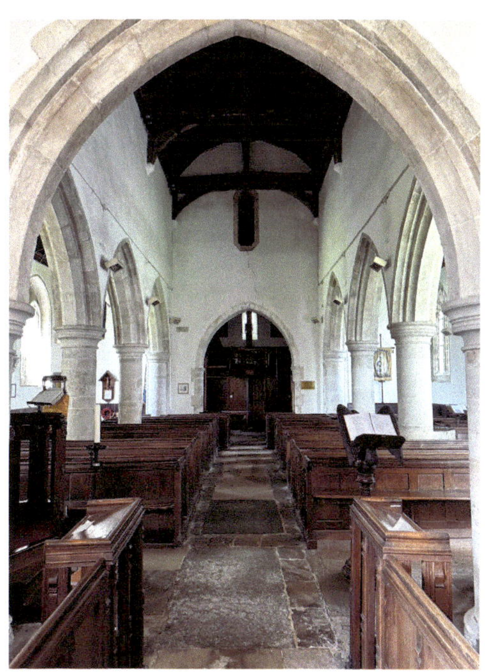

39. SOUTHEASE, NO KNOWN DEDICATION

Sussex has three churches with round towers. The other two are at Piddinghoe and St Michael in Lewes. We now think this was a fashion imported from Scandinavia – the vast majority of English round towers being in East Anglia, with which there was direct trade. They date from late Saxon times to the fourteenth century. This one is especially pretty as it has a conical roof. Inside we find that the chancel arch is timber and that the wall separating nave and chancel is not stone but timber framed. In the late medieval period, the original chancel was demolished, probably because it was slipping downhill and the original Saxon nave was shortened by the addition of this partition to create a small chancel. Fragments of wall paintings survive throughout the church, but it is difficult to pick out many scenes. On the west wall at eye level there are several consecration crosses, each relating to a different period of rebuilding, which mark where the Bishop anointed the building with Holy Oil. On the north wall a blocked Saxon window sits above the thirteenth-century window that replaced it. The charming organ dates from the eighteenth century. This very simple interior with muted tones is relieved by two stained-glass windows. In the chancel is a very jazzy design left to us by the Victorians incorporating the Alpha and Omega symbols. At the west end of the church is an abstract window by Marguerite Douglas-Thompson, a Sussex artist who worked for the Lowndes and Drury studio who also designed a window at neighbouring Piddinghoe church.

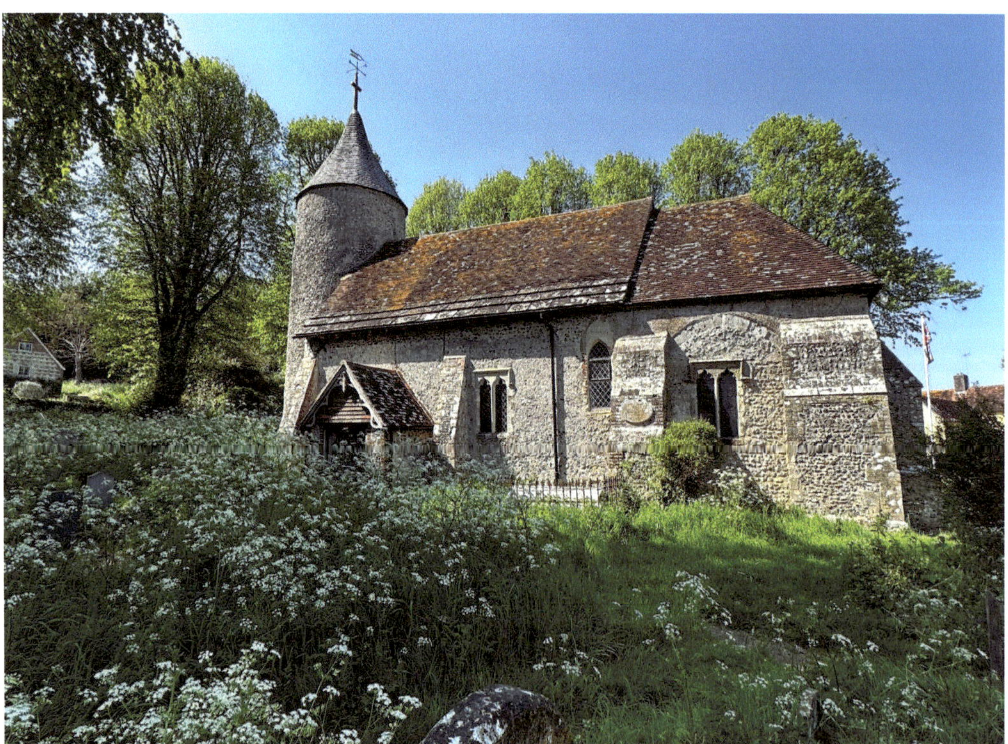

Southease. One of three surviving round-towered churches in East Sussex. The large buttress at the east end reminds us that building on a hillside can often be problematic and that the east end here has been considerably shortened.

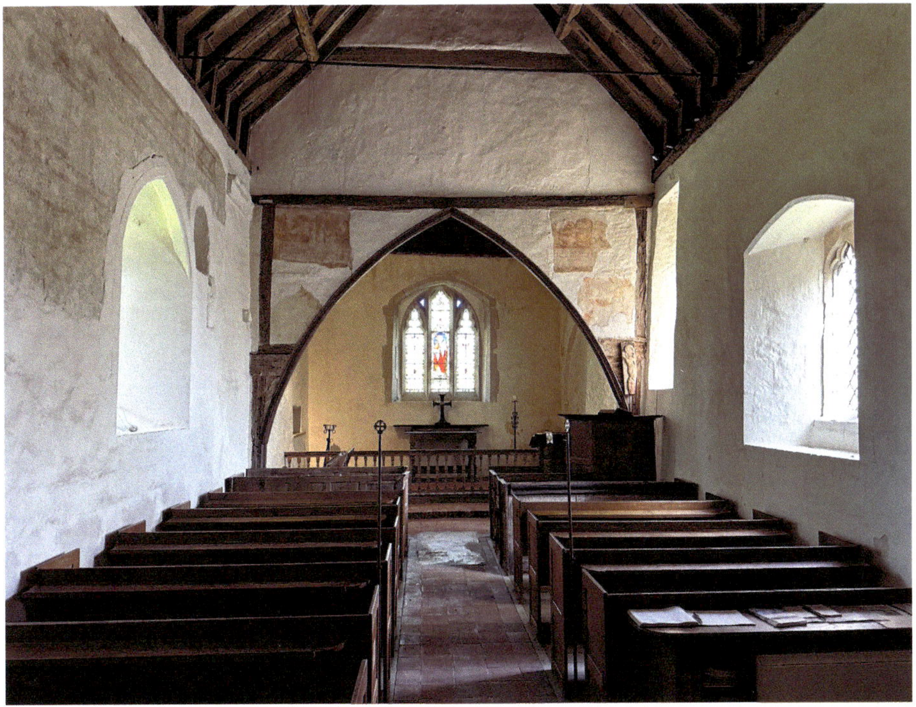

Southease. The chancel arch and wall above are formed of timber rather than stone and lead into a shortened chancel, the result of structural issues.

40. STREAT, NO DEDICATION KNOWN

A lovely setting on high ground looking south towards the South Downs. The church is mainly nineteenth century but contains older objects. The earliest are two cast-iron ledger slabs in the central gangway. One is enormous and records several members of the eighteenth-century Gott family. It was one of the last of its type as the local forges which produced them were closing as a result of greater industrialisation. The smaller slab is of 1731 (the 3 got reversed in casting) and is to the daughter of a resident of Wadhurst, the church of which has the largest number of these memorials (see entry). Above them are two massive wall monuments of multicoloured marbles to the Dobell family. One records that Mrs Dobell had been an heiress, so no wonder these memorials are on such a scale. In the south aisle are three stained-glass windows of a recognisable style. They appear to be the work of Charles Eamer Kempe, the Sussex-born designer of 7,000 church windows whose work we find in over forty Sussex churches. However, they are not by him, but by one of his pupils, H. W. Bryans. When Bryans realised that Kempe's windows were so popular, he left the firm and set up his own studio producing near identical windows at a cheaper price. To the layman it is difficult to tell the difference unless they are signed. Kempe used the wheatsheaf whilst Bryans had a greyhound which usually appears at the end of the text box. In the north wall is a later memorial window by Hugh Powell which incorporates horses, a mallard, kingfisher and an orange budgerigar!

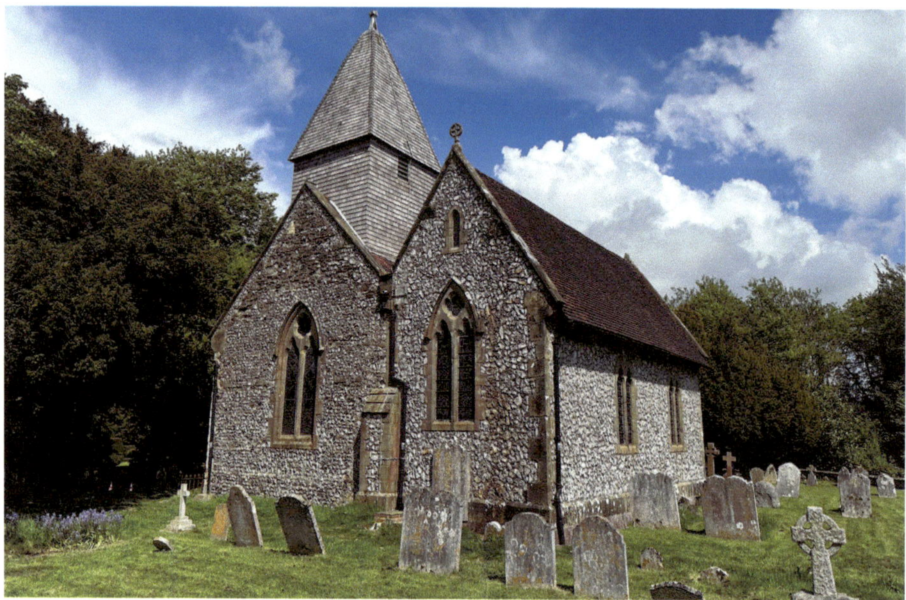

Streat. A Norman church onto which the Victorians added a south aisle with its own roof structure. Their walls are laid like crazy paving whilst the medieval walls are laid in horizontal courses.

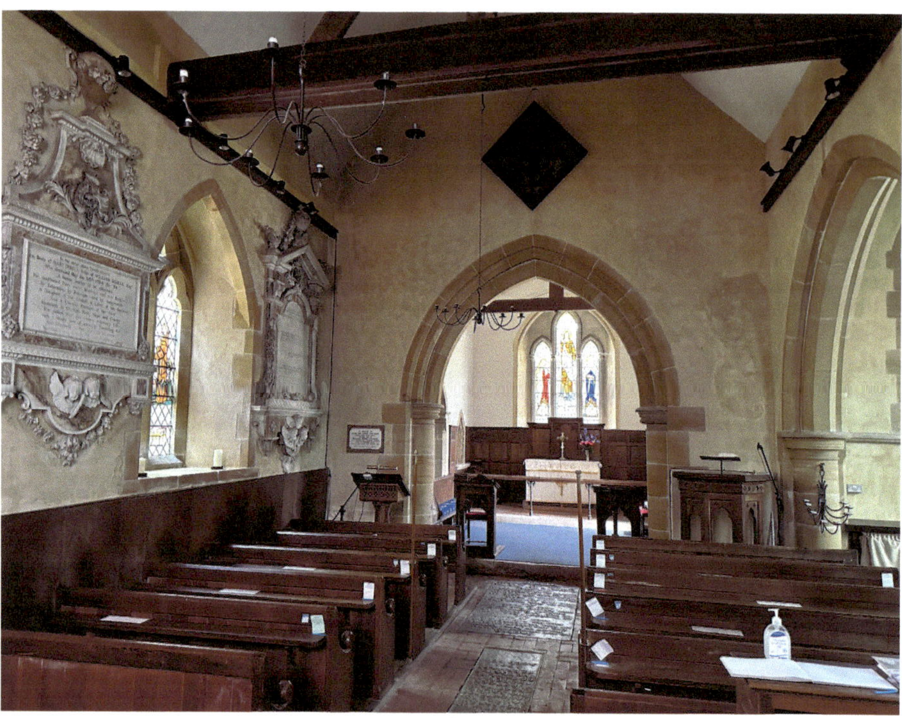

Streat. This simple interior is given character by the two huge monuments to the Dobell family. The royal arms over the chancel arch are those of Charles II, dated 1660.

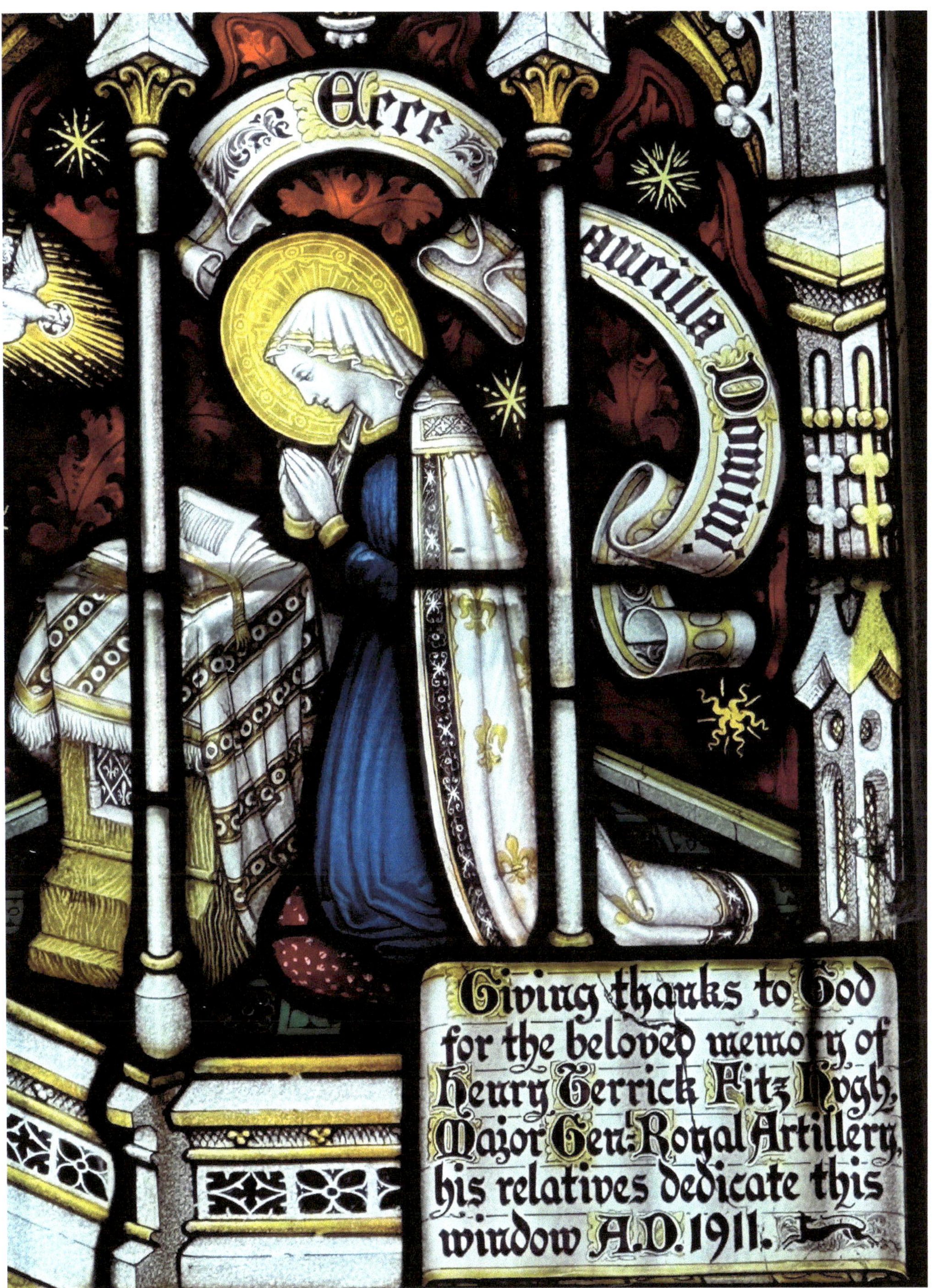

Streat. This window in the style of Kempe is by H. W. Bryans, as can be seen from his signature of a greyhound at the end of the text box.

41. TICEHURST, ST MARY

This church was built in the tumultuous years following the Black Death, although the large clerestory windows that allow so much light into the church are a nineteenth-century intervention. The upper opening of the rood loft staircase can be seen on the north side of the chancel arch, but the twentieth-century screen was built on a grander scale than its medieval predecessor and the levels do not line up. The star of the interior is the Tudor font cover with eight sides, four of which open to reveal elaborate tracery carved on the inner faces as well. It was obviously a gift to the church from a private donor and whilst much of the inscription has been lost, the name Elizabeth is easy to pick out. In the north aisle we can find the Decalogue, Creed and Lord's Prayer painted on canvas which were originally displayed on the east wall. They are signed by John Marten and dated 1764. Marten painted at least five surviving works in Kent and Sussex churches and also produced church memorials. Nearby is an oddity – a Sussex Smock made a hundred years ago by members of the local WI. The north chapel contains a sturdy ebonised bier and many memorials to the Courthope family. The tie beam supporting its medieval crownpost roof split under the strain of movement many centuries ago and was very crudely repaired with iron ties. The wide reredos in the chancel is by Martin Travers (see also Wadhurst) and next to it outstanding fragments of medieval stained glass include a

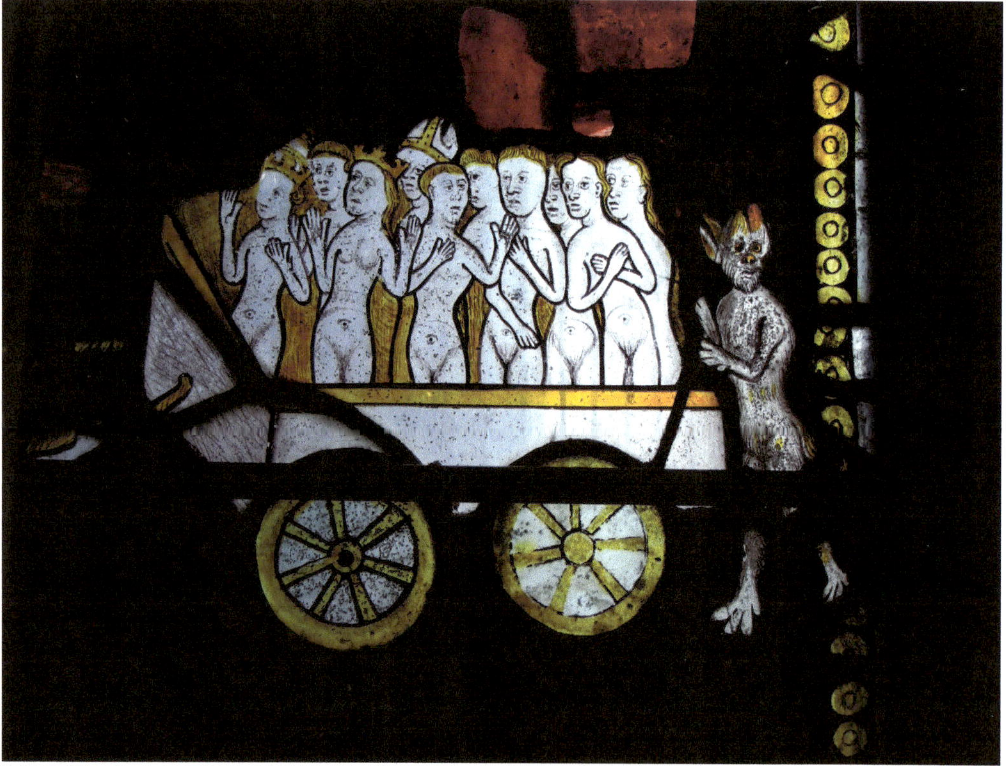

Ticehurst. This fragment of medieval glass shows part of the 'Doom' scene and depicts lost souls being taken by handcart to the Jaws of Hell.

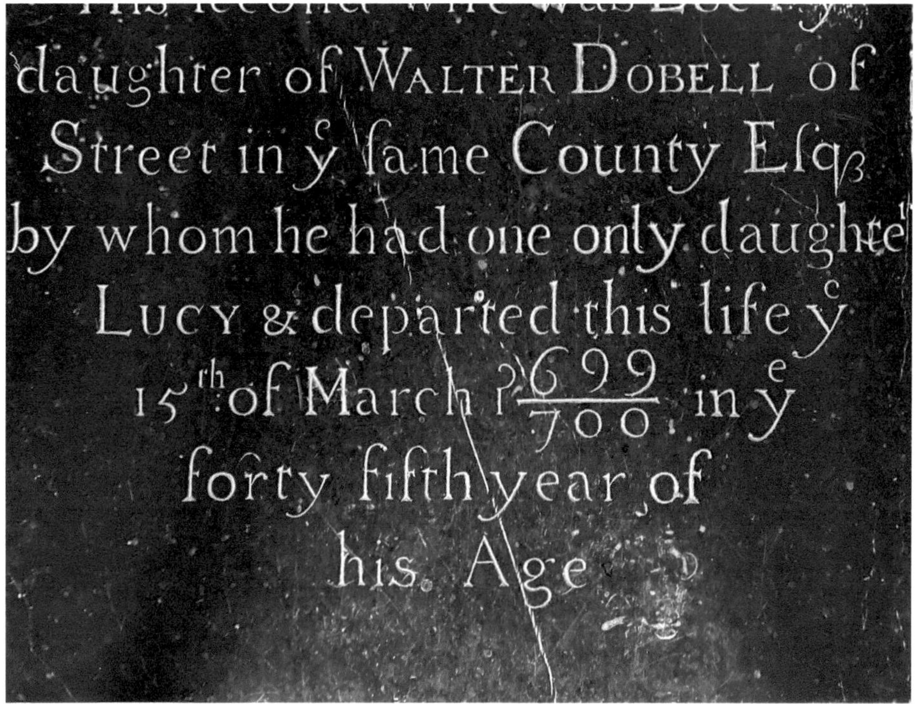

Ticehurst. From 1582 until 1752 we used two calendars, the Julian and Gregorian, and anything that occurred in the first three months of the year would be recorded as being in both years.

scene showing the souls of the lost being taken to Hell in a handcart. It is gratifying to see that a pope and a bishop are amongst those 'going down'. In the centre of the chancel is a black marble ledger slab to Walter and Lucy Roberts. Lucy died in March 1700 when both the Julian and Gregorian calendars were in popular use, which is why her death is also recorded as March 1699 (the first three months of the year were counted in both calendars from 1582 to 1752 when the Gregorian calendar was finally adopted in Britain).

42. TORTINGTON, ST MARY MAGDALENE

Another one of the county's retired churches, this romantic Norman building stands behind a farmyard and may be located by its painted bellcote peeping over the barns. The church consists of nave and chancel with a south aisle which sits under a catslide roof. This aisle has had a chequered history for it was built in the thirteenth century, demolished in the seventeenth and rebuilt in the nineteenth! Even more remarkable is its south doorway, for this was part of the original Norman church, which was moved to its present position when the aisle was built, moved back when the aisle was demolished and incorporated again when the aisle was rebuilt. It is a much-travelled doorway, like all the dressed stone in the church, carved from Caen stone imported from France. Just inside the door is the font, another example of carving of the Romanesque period, with huge acanthus leaf pendants from its cable-moulded rim. You can see the damage where an iron hinge was inserted to hold a later lid. The nave is very dark as the addition of the south aisle took the windows away from the centre of the building – you can see why later churches often incorporated clerestory windows. The visitor comes here primarily to see the chancel arch which is carved with amazing boggle-eyed monsters known as beakheads. They take the form of comical birds' faces with their beaks wrapped around the roll moulding of the arch. Common in further-flung parts of the country, they are found in just two other Sussex churches. Imagine what they must have been like when brightly painted in primary colours. The stunning glass in the tiny east window shows the Lamb of God and the symbols of the Four Evangelists and is by Thomas Willement, one of the most important men in the development of nineteenth-century stained glass, who was able to perfect glass production as it had been in the medieval period. It dates from 1836 and was commissioned by the rector. The side windows of the chancel take the form of a grisaille design, based on thirteenth-century originals. They too are Victorian and were made in Arundel by a local glass painter, Mr Wright.

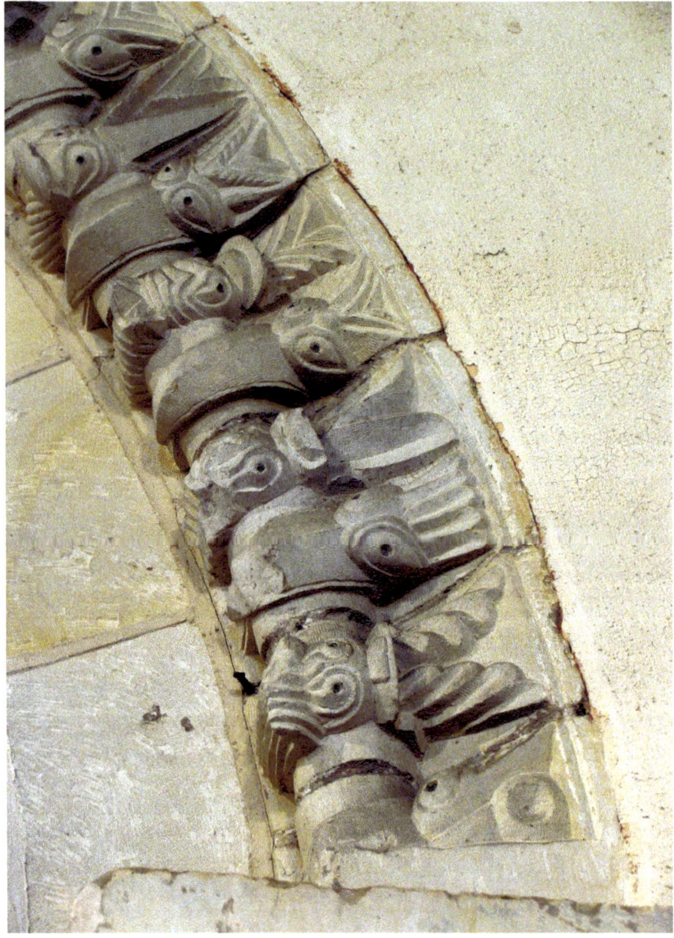

Tortington. The Norman chancel arch is carved with beakhead decoration. Here the cartoon-like birds' beaks are designed to bite onto the circular moulding of the arch.

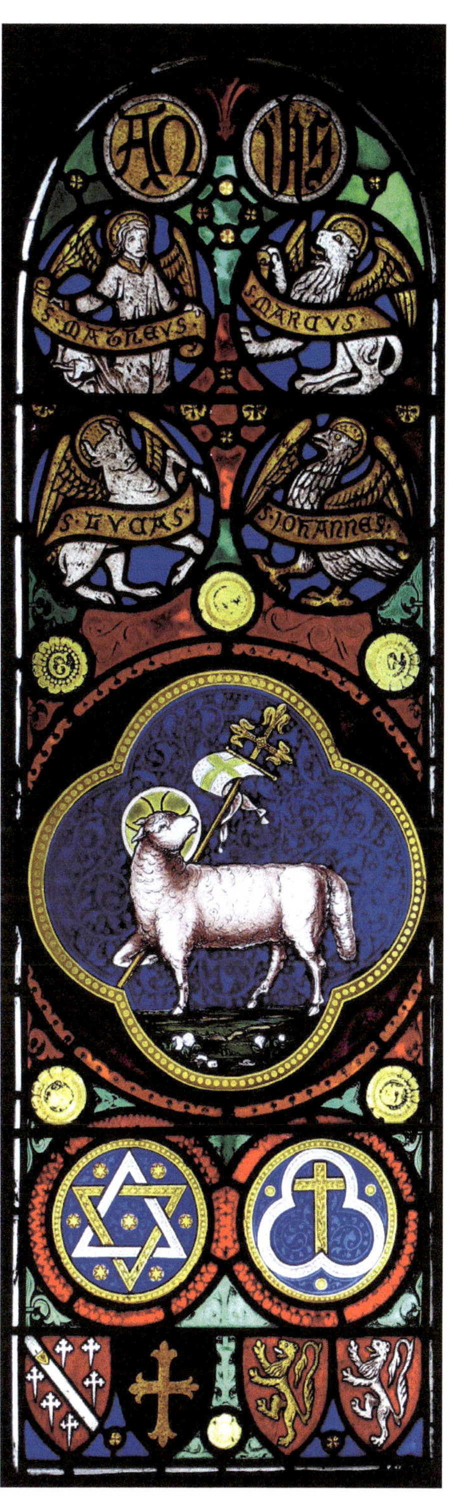

Tortington. This colourful glass in the east window dates from 1836 and was designed by Thomas Willement, who had rediscovered medieval techniques of stained-glass production.

43. WADHURST, ST PETER AND ST PAUL

Set back from the High Street and effectively closed off from it by buildings, this church has seen many alterations over the years, although its Norman tower retains many of its original round-headed openings. The church is built of sandstone and each separate building campaign used a slightly different building technique – larger blocks, squared blocks, more mortar, so even if you cannot identify the periods involved, it is easy to differentiate them. I'd recommend standing by the west wall of the south aisle where you get the full range of techniques. The west doorway of the tower has been replaced and displays the initials of the churchwardens responsible and the year 1812 inset into the roundels. You enter by the south porch with a lovely octopartite vault with a boss of the Holy Name in the centre. Vaulted porches can mean only one thing – a room above, and the staircase to it may be found just to the left as you go into the church. Money was left to its construction in 1402. It is rare to find post-Reformation burials in a porch but here is the vault of the Luck family with three fine eighteenth-century memorials, two of which incorporate the regional speciality, terracotta plaques by the Harmer family of Heathfield. The church is wide and light and in the main dates from the thirteenth century, with round and octagonal piers, and a horizontal string course around the chancel walls. It is best known for its

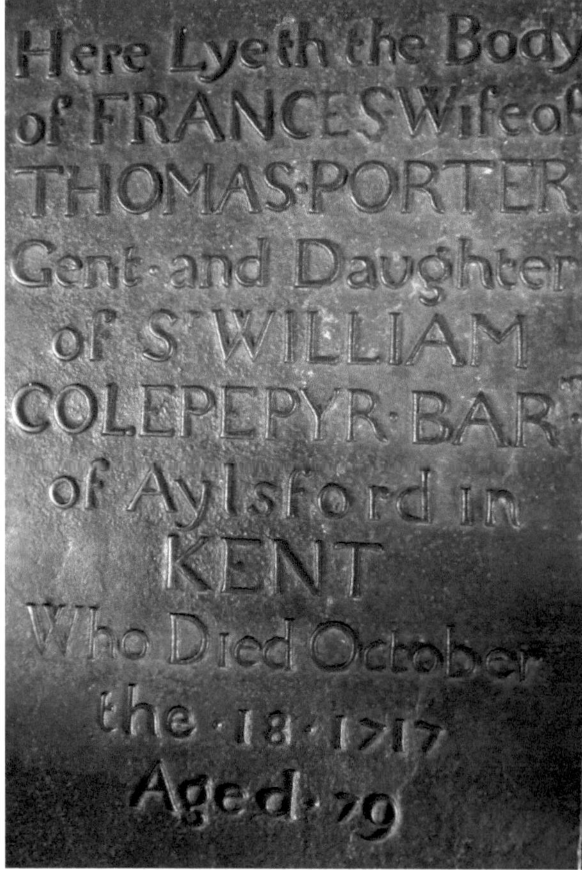

Wadhurst. This church has the largest number of cast-iron grave slabs in the country, reflecting the importance of the forges in this parish.

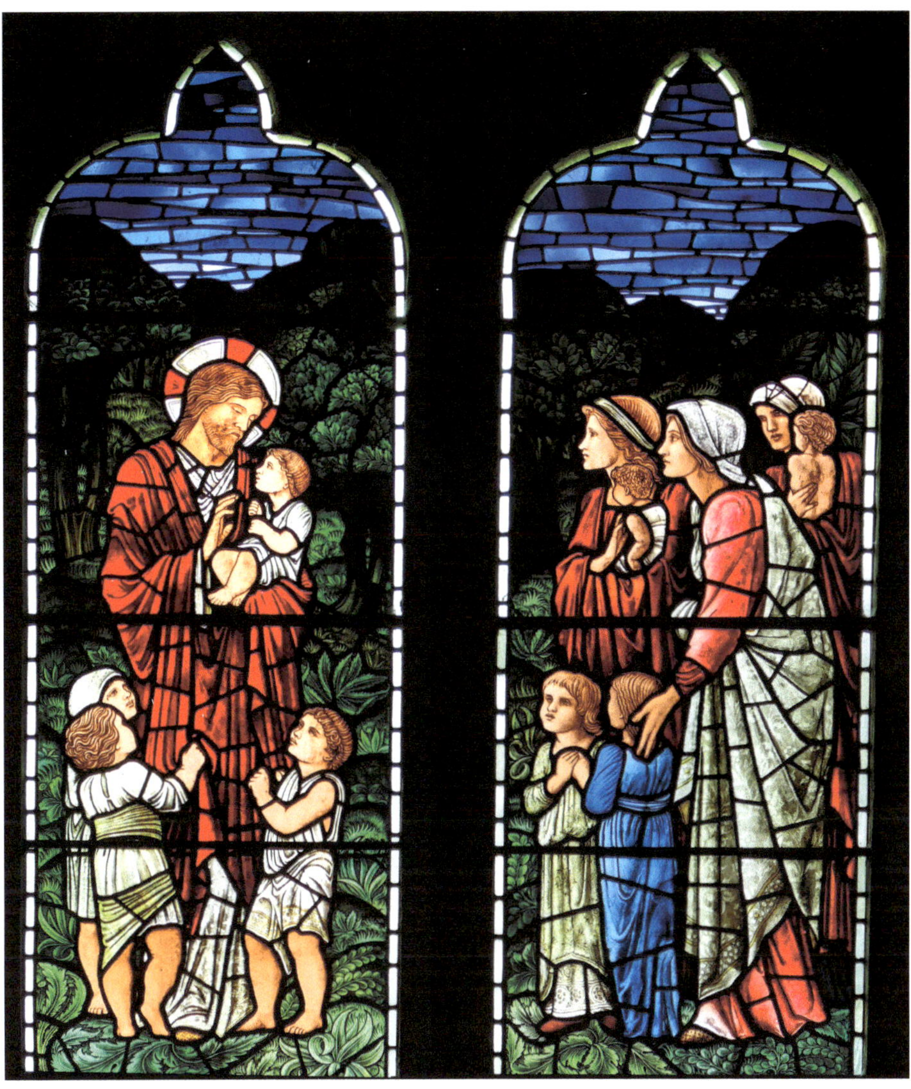

Wadhurst. This window is by the firm of Morris and Co. with its typically striated leadwork.

amazing collection of cast-iron grave slabs made locally when smelting was the main industry. There are thirty-one in total and you could spend hours studying them. At the east end of the south aisle is a fine twentieth-century altarpiece of Christ Rising from the Tomb designed by Martin Travers and painted by one of his pupils. The screen at the base of the tower is another charming twentieth-century piece, in iron, with gambling lambs and Sussex martlets, hops and local wild plants. In the chancel the piscina and sedilia (no more than a lowered windowsill), low to the floor, show how much the floor level of this end of the church was raised by the Victorians. On your way out admire the delightful window by Morris and Co. at the west end of the south aisle.

44. Warbleton, St Mary

Serving a scattered community, this is one of those churches you can return to time and again and always find something new to see. Mainly thirteenth century with a fourteenth-century north aisle and fifteenth-century tower it is built on high ground with little more than a pub and former workhouse for company. Right at the top of the tower is a fine corbel table of projecting heads designed to frighten away evil spirits. As soon as you enter you are confronted by the huge private manorial gallery which occupies much of the north aisle, dated on the front 1722 and divided into two sections – the front seats for the Lord of the Manor and the rear section for his servants. Its imposing staircase rises from near the north door where, no doubt, he made his entrance. Incidentally, the north door still has its locking pole of wood which runs into the hollow wall and which stops the door being broken down from outside. Above the gallery are two diamond-shaped hatchments carried at the

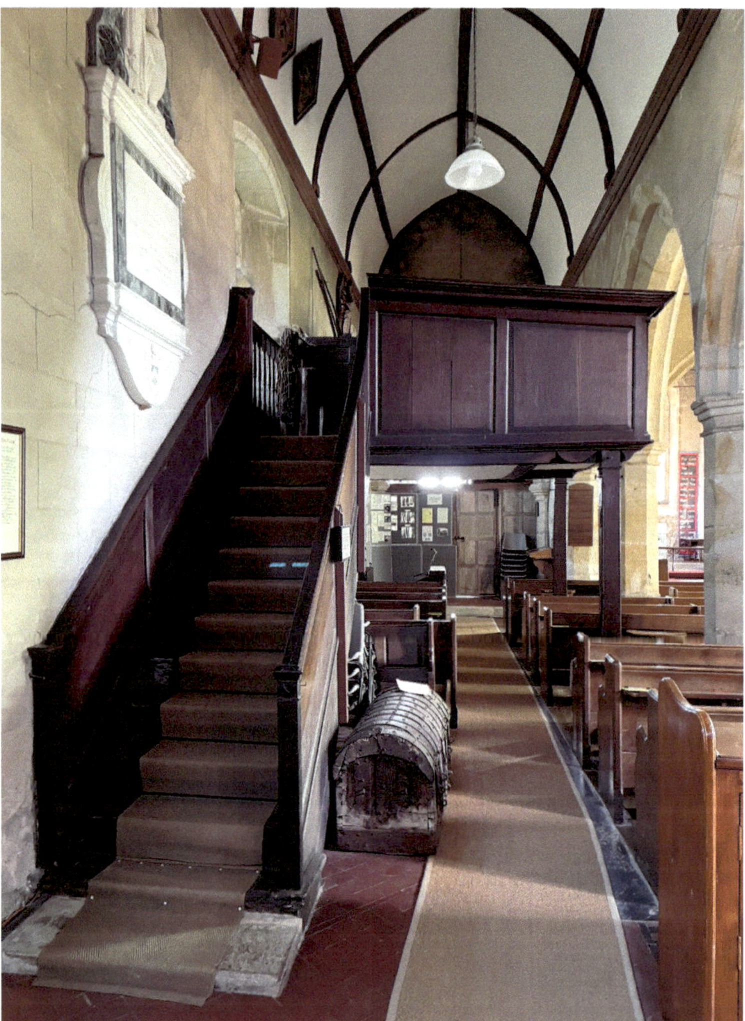

Left: Warbleton. The private gallery and staircase in the north aisle was a status symbol erected in 1722. The seating area up there is divided into two sections.

Opposite: Warbleton. The brass of William Prestwyck, who died in 1436, is in the centre of the chancel, a location that was his prerogative as incumbent of the parish.

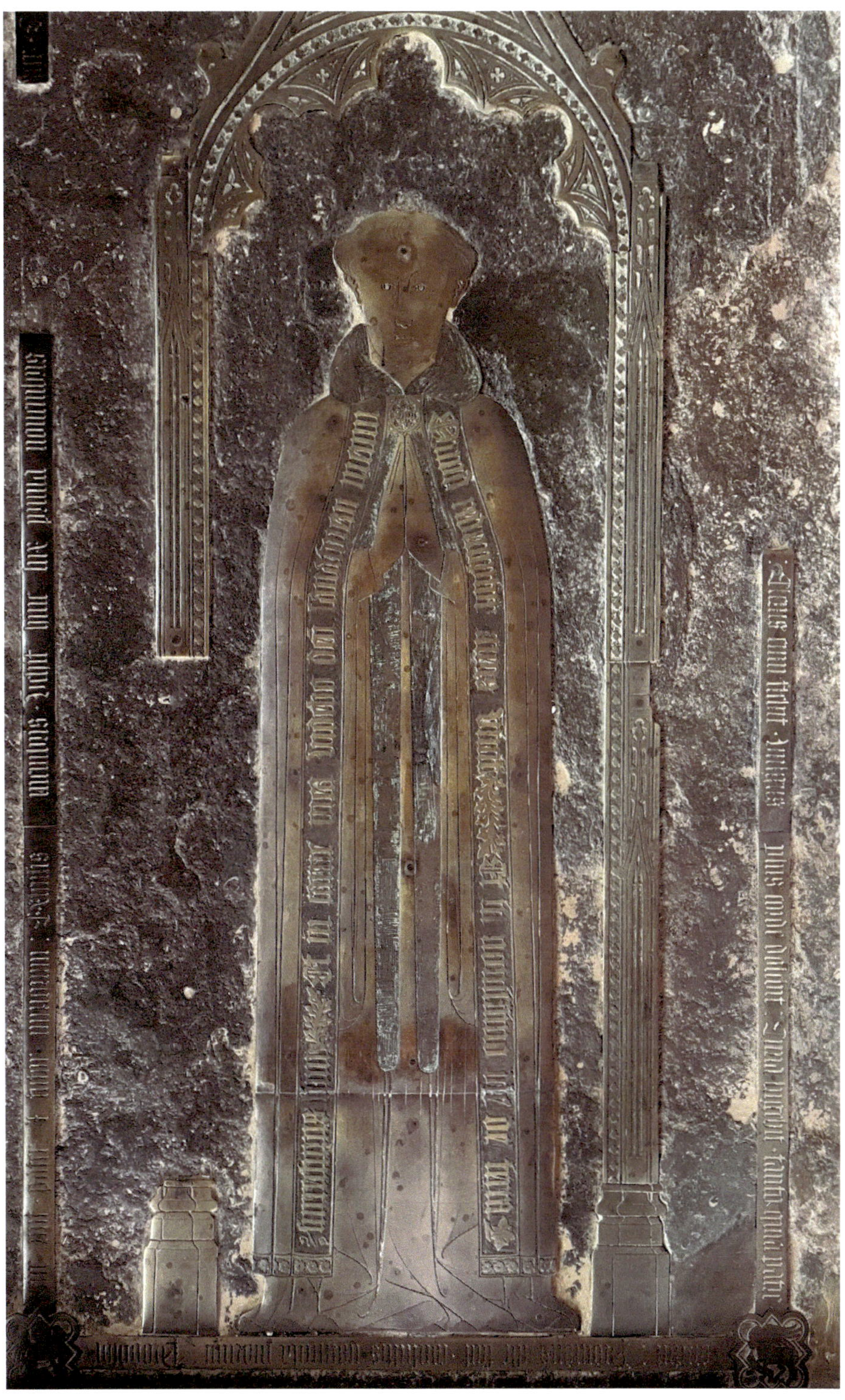

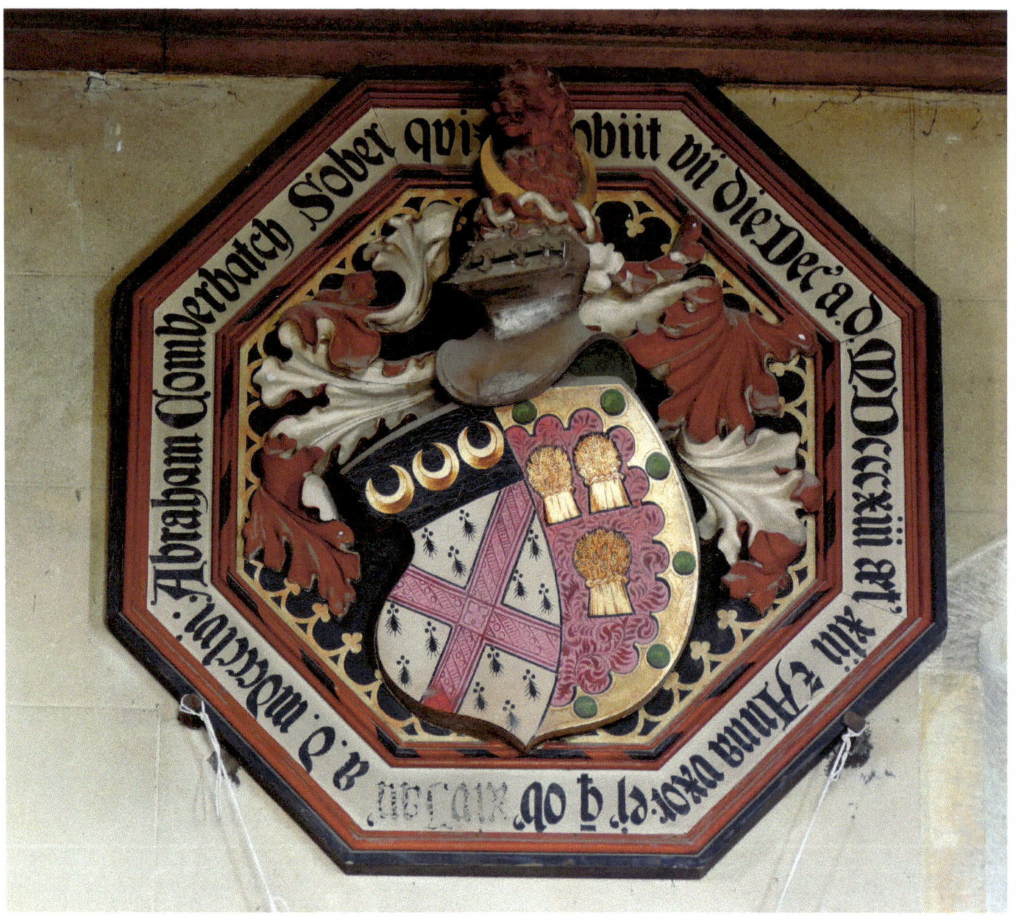

Warbleton. This hatchment is by Charles Eamer Kempe and was made around seventy-five years after the death of the person it commemorates, who was a distant relative of Kempe.

funerals of the Revd and Mrs Henry Harcourt (d. 1800 and 1796 respectively). To the east is a more unusual hatchment, octagonal in shape, to Abraham Comberbatch Sober who was married to Anne Kempe, whose cousin, Charles Eamer Kempe, undoubtedly designed this in the late nineteenth century as a retrospective memorial. Similar examples by him are to be found at Lindfield church, too. Under the carpet in the chancel is a huge brass to a priest, William Prestwyck (d. 1436), with the text 'I know that My Redeemer Liveth' engraved along the orphrey of his robes. The church chest is domed in shape and is one of a series to have come from the Baltic coast in the fifteenth century. Hidden behind the organ is one of the county's finest eighteenth-century memorials which commemorates Sir John Lade (d. 1740) who, if we are to believe the inscription, was an all-round good guy who did 'great favours to his friends', although his portrait bust gives him a rather severe appearance. Look out for the graffiti on the clear glass here which tells us that it was installed by 'Samuel Farmer of Burwash, April 7th 1753'.

45. WARMINGHURST, THE HOLY SEPULCHRE

The vast majority of medieval churches in Sussex are composed of, at least, a nave and separate chancel, but here is an example of a single-cell building of thirteenth-century date where nave and chancel fitted into a simple rectangular box. Its light interior is famous for being filled with eighteenth-century furnishings, almost untouched by Victorian restorers, but there is much more to it than that. The church is mainly built of unpolished Sussex marble with the lower courses of its roof in Horsham slab. The corners of the building were formed of greensand, whilst the main doorways are of Caen stone and came from elsewhere. This is where it gets interesting. The big house of the area stood in the field to the west of the church and was granted in 1540 to the Shelley family by Henry VIII. No doubt the Shelleys carried out renewals and renovations to their new home. In 1676 the house was sold to William Penn who went on to found Pennsylvania and shortly afterwards it was sold to James Butler who demolished it. It is highly likely that the Caen stone doorways now in the church were originally in the Shelley house as they are of a domestic character and were reused in the church by the Butlers. Walking around the outside, the careful observer will notice filled-in putlog holes where the original wooden scaffolding was built into the wall along the north side of the church. Here too is the early seventeenth-century

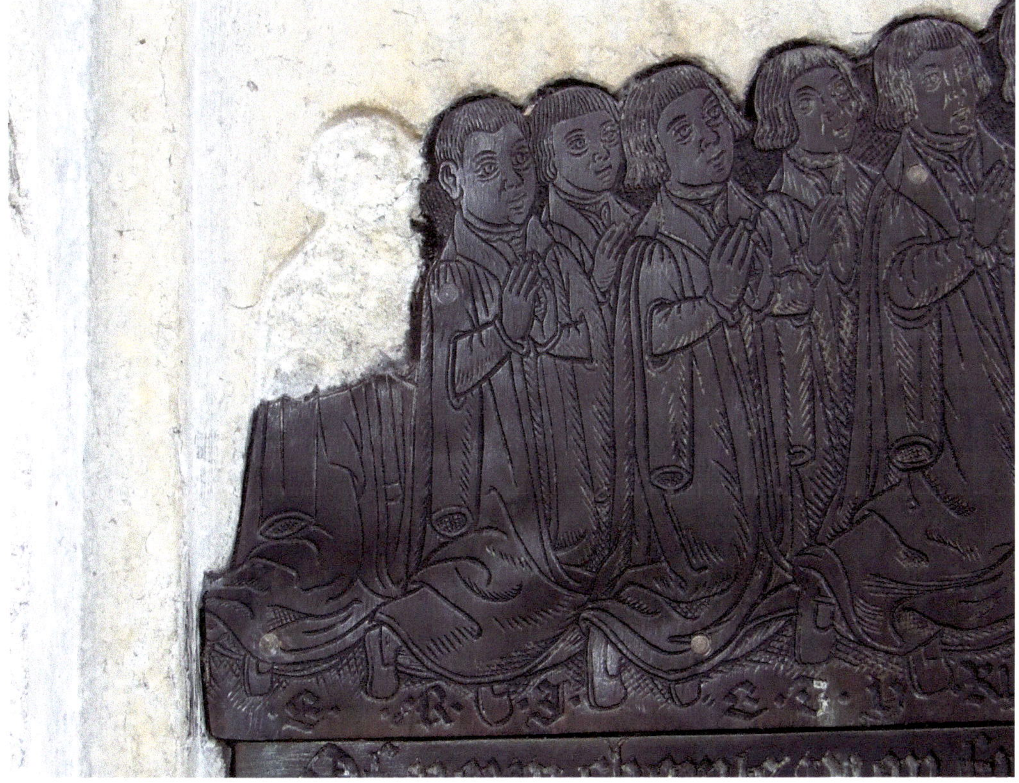

Warminghurst. This is a detail of the Shelley brass which clearly shows that Edward Shelley has been deliberately removed, possibly after his execution in 1588.

mausoleum of the Shelley family, complete with a window that must also have come from their house. On the south side of the church an eighteenth-century (former) porch blocks a complete circumnavigation of the building. As you enter through the west door look above, and you will see that a large window has been blocked in immediately above the door. There were probably fears that the bellcote, the woodwork of which has been dendro-dated to 1158, was too heavy and causing the window to buckle. Incidentally, the bell is one of the oldest in the county, cast in around 1200. The pews and benches inside, together with the chancel screen, are eighteenth century. The latter carries the royal arms of Queen Anne with her personal motto of 'Semper Eadem' (always the same). Don't be confused by the date 1845 in the bottom corner, as this refers to a Victorian repainting! Beneath the two-decker pulpit is a very wide chair for the parish clerk, who must have been broad in the beam. In the chancel are the memorials to the families who owned the manor, the most interesting of which is on the north wall. It takes the form of a brass to Edward and Joan Shelley, made by the Fermer workshop in London in the 1550s. Although it has lost its image of the Holy Trinity and its heraldic shields, it retains images of the ten Shelley children, each with their initial clearly inscribed beneath. However, the left-hand image, of son Edward, has been deliberately cut off with a knife, and it is supposed that this was done after his execution at Tyburn in 1588. He was martyred for his Catholic faith, so perhaps some local protestant decided to obliterate his memory or it is possible that a herald from London was sent down. The later monuments in the chancel are to the Butler family who created the church interior as we see it today.

46. WEST CHILTINGTON

This welcoming church stands on high ground near the centre of the village where – by the churchyard gate – are the village stocks, now a rare feature but 150 years ago found in every parish. The tower stands in an unusual position, over the east end of the nave, and is supported by a large internal wooden frame which displays the year 1602. The church is renowned for its wall paintings which represent a series of medieval schemes. There are some interesting figurative scenes depicting the Passion of Christ, delightful foliage to the right of the chancel arch and jazzy designs on the underside of the arcades. What we see is substantial but at one time there was even more. Architecturally I've always been taken by the window in the south wall where there is a niche which would once have contained the image of a saint. It's a very simple pointed recess but look carefully and you will see that around it is painted a much more elaborate fictive arch complete with pinnacles! Incidentally, the windowsill also displays a fragment of Romanesque sculpture. From here you can see a feature easily missed. Look above the arch into the south chapel and there is a painted Gordian knot. No doubt it's there to catch evil spirits. Below it is a hagioscope which once gave a priest in the south aisle a view of the altar, whilst in front of it is an Ellacombe chiming system designed so that one person can chime all the bells. The wire has been fed through the doorway that formerly carried the rood loft across the chancel arch! In the chancel is a small brass plaque recording the death of Robert Johnson who was parson here for over fifty years and who we are told lived long enough to see his great-great-grandchildren.

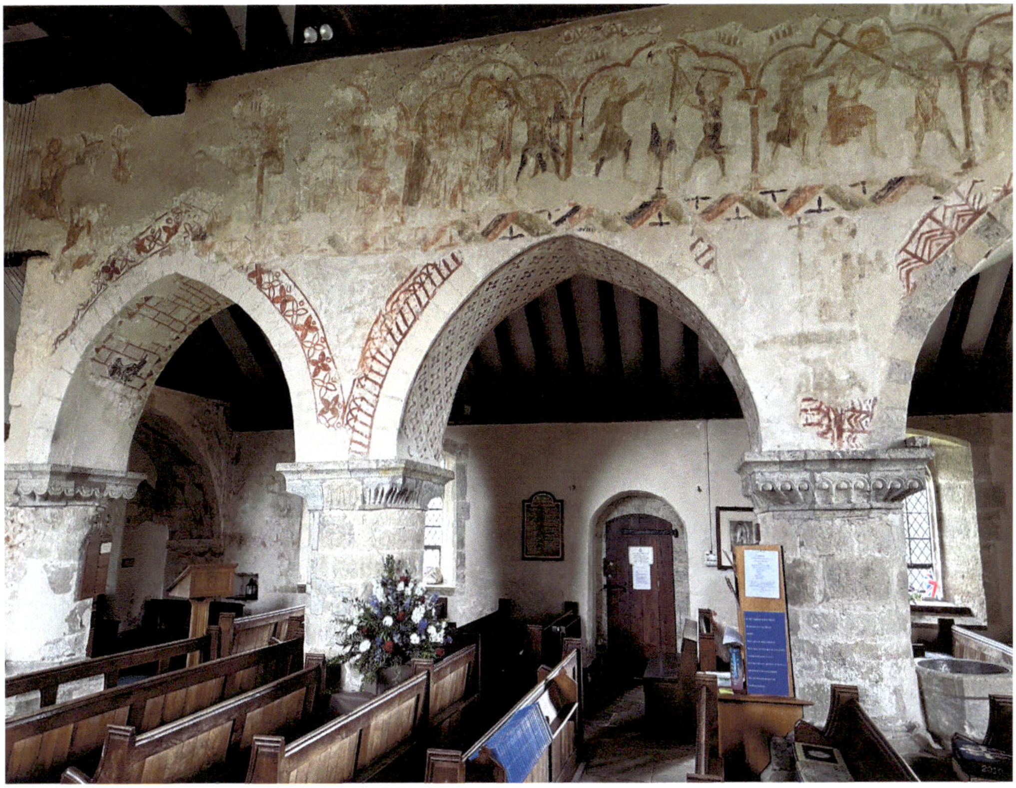

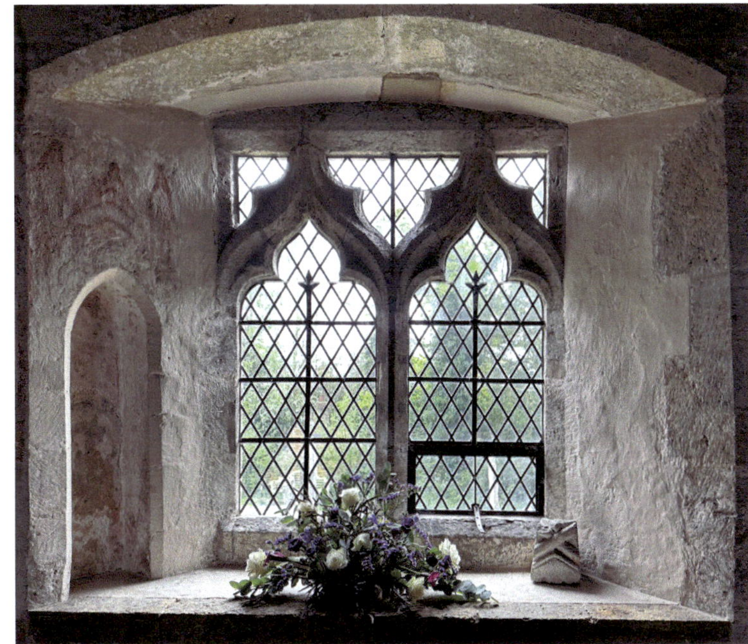

Above: West Chiltington. Here the wall paintings are in narrative layers and the arcades are also decorated to emphasise their shapes. One series of paintings overlays the other.

Right: West Chiltington. This window in the south aisle was built as a commemorative piece as its frame contains a niche for a statue which in turn is surrounded by a more elaborate fictive niche painting.

47. WEST GRINSTEAD, ST GEORGE

Seemingly in a remote location, but within earshot of the A24, the church is approached from the north and at once presents its thirteenth-century heyday in the form of single lancet windows in the chancel. The roof is covered with large Horsham slabs which are also used on the lower levels of the broach spire, and on the rectangular porch. The core of the building is Norman but so completely was it remodelled in the thirteenth century that this is now the abiding memory, together with the fact that the tower stands as part of a linear progression of south aisle, tower and south chancel chapel. It is a building brimming with interesting furnishings. The front benches in the nave are unusual in having the names of the houses to which they were allocated painted on them with archaic names like Grinders, Fullers and

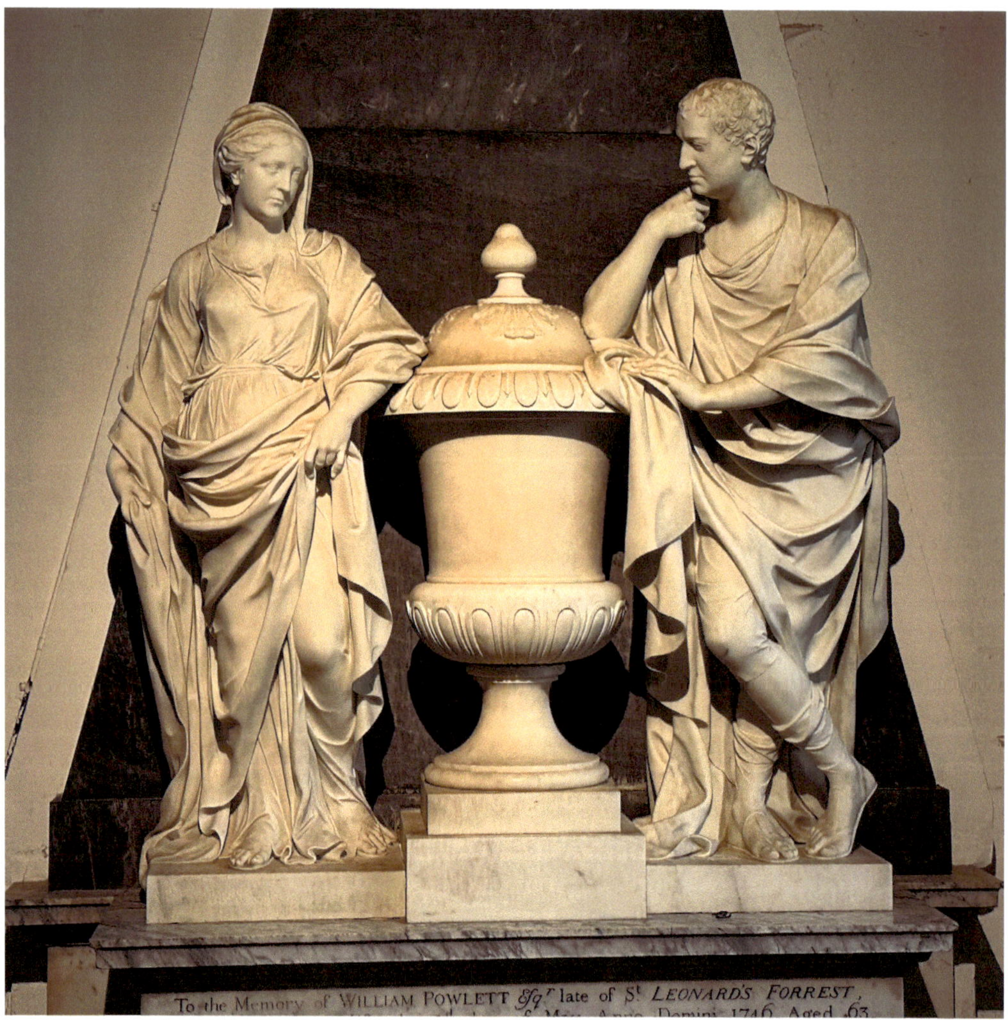

West Grinstead. The memorial signed by Michael Rysbrack to the Powlett family dates from the mid-eighteenth century.

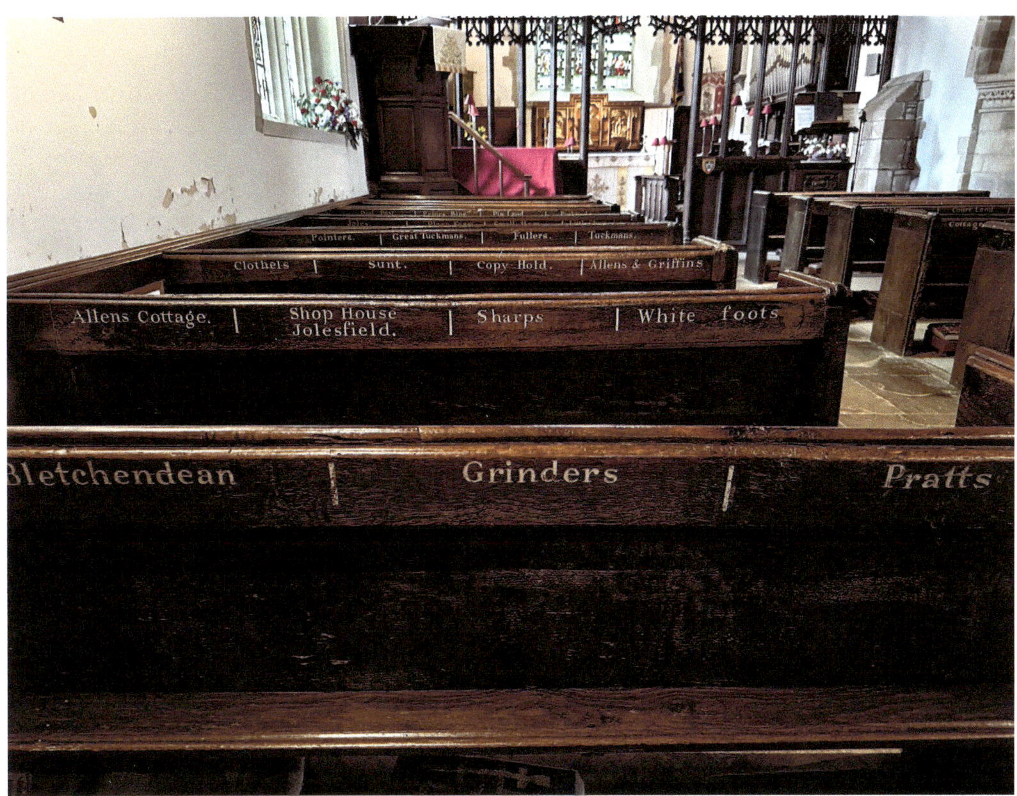

West Grinstead. The benches bear the names of the houses to which the seats were allocated in accordance to how much pew rent the occupiers had paid. This was once a common way for churches to increase their income.

Pin Land. Following the Reformation churches used pew rents to offset their expenses and sometimes the whole church was filled with rented seats. Apart from this church, only that at Shermanbury displays benches like this in Sussex. The south arcade is thirteenth century in date with characteristic round piers and plain mouldings, although the arch to the tower base has some rather good moulded capitals. The pulpit and sounding board date from the seventeenth century and stand in front of a twentieth-century rood screen – the main division between nave and chancel, as there is no chancel arch. Off the chancel is a south chapel now used as a vestry and organ chamber which contains two Sussex marble slabs raised off the floor and each displaying a memorial brass to the Halsham family. Under the tower is a finely carved portrait bust of Sir Merrick Burrell which depicts a jowly man with a well-made wig. The Burrells are still the main landowners in the area. Even more spectacular is the monument by Michael Rysbrack which stands at the west end of the south aisle. This has life-size depictions of Elizabeth and William Powlett (d. 1746 and 1753). Rysbrack's signature is not very prominent but can be found below Elizabeth's feet. There is also some good glass here. By the pulpit is a typical window by Charles Eamer Kempe depicting three saints including St Catherine who holds the broken wheel by which she should have been killed had not a miracle occurred. In the south aisle is a window by Carl Edwards (1967), in the left-hand light of which you will see the church, whilst the stunning west window is by Walter Camm in the Arts and Crafts style of 1922.

48. WEST HOATHLY, ST MARGARET OF ANTIOCH

A picture-postcard village full of interesting houses, amongst them the medieval Priest House which is open to the public. From there many visitors explore the nearby parish church, a Norman building extended in the thirteenth and fourteenth centuries. In your eagerness to get inside don't miss the south door which is decorated with the date March 31 1626 in nails. One can only suppose that on that Friday they proudly installed the new door! The interior has been reordered and is very well cared for. The earliest feature is the font, which is of local marble and dates from the Norman period, supported on five round pillars. In the north wall is a stunning stained-glass window by Douglas Strachan (see also Winchelsea) of 1927 depicting King David, St George and farm labourers with angels ascending to the golden light of Heaven. It's a memorial to Kenneth Arbuthnot killed at the Battle of Ypres. The thirteenth-century windows in the north wall of the chancel were rather expensive in their day with decorative attached shafts and painted foliate wall decoration, much of which survives. No doubt of the same date is the en-suite piscina and sedilia of three equal seats. Above them it's easy to see a half-arch, twin

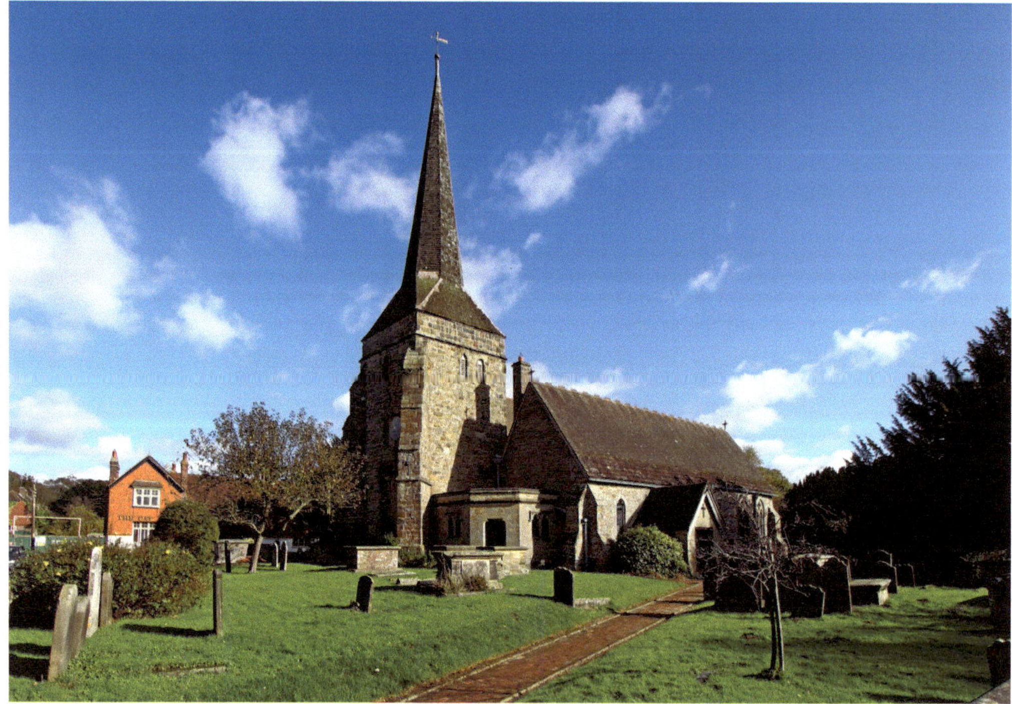

West Hoathly. This prominent spire may be found in other East Sussex churches where the Wealden forest provided unlimited supplies of timber.

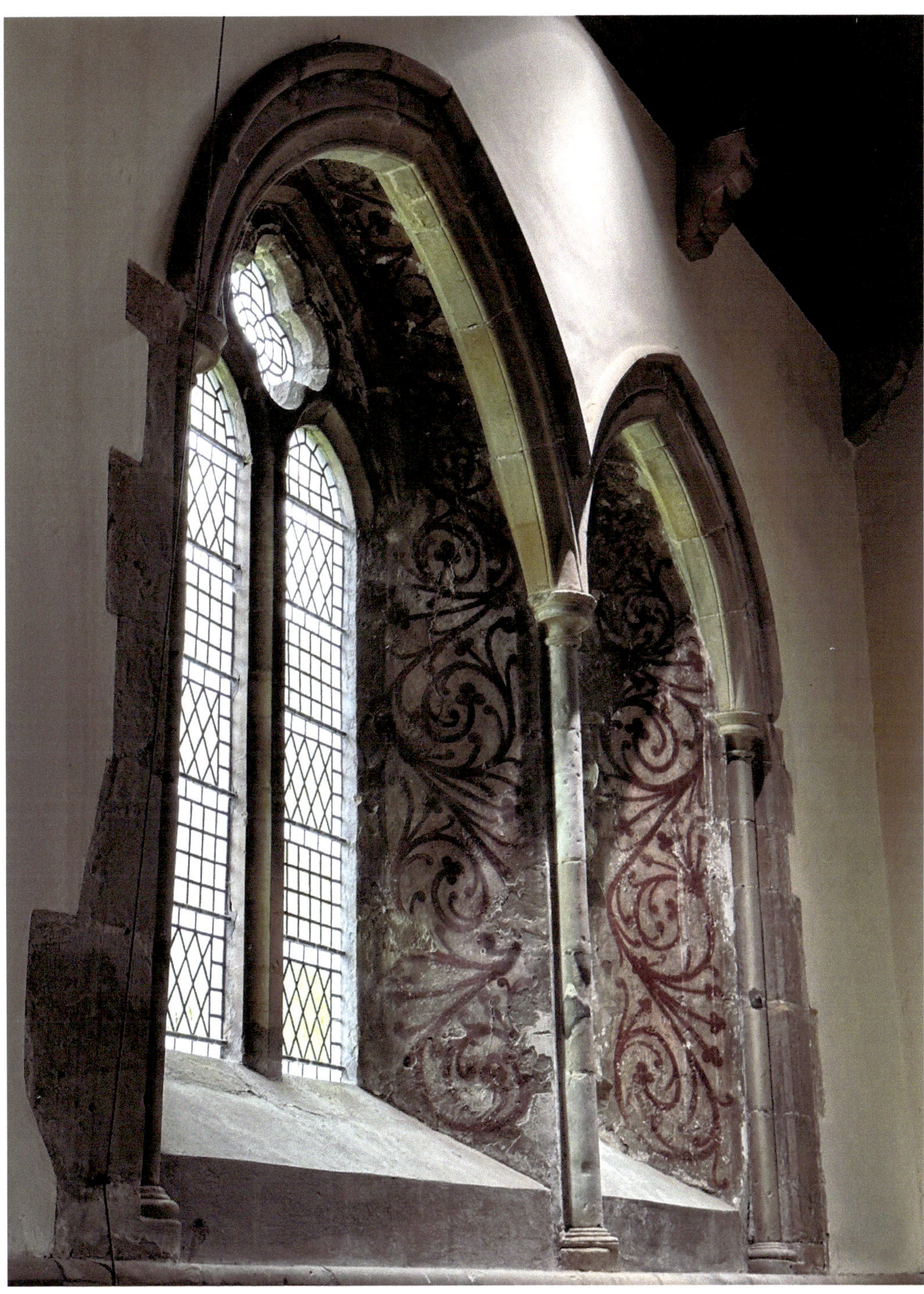

West Hoathly. In the chancel these thirteenth-century lancet windows have carved rere-arches on the inside face of the wall as well as their original foliate painted design.

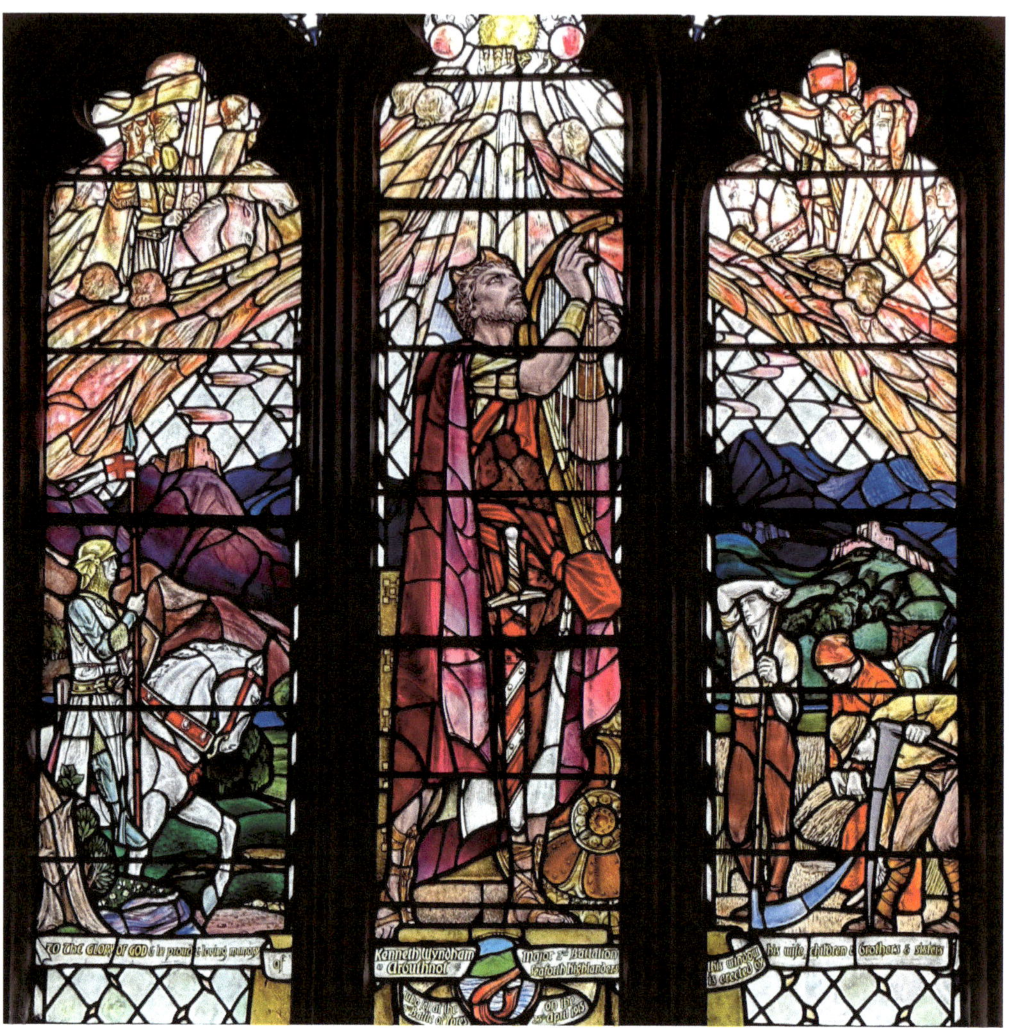

West Hoathly. This window of 1921 was designed by Douglas Strachan whose more famous Sussex windows are at Winchelsea. Here we see King David and St George.

to the one opposite, which lost its window when the south aisle was extended into a chapel in the fourteenth century. Against the wall in the south aisle are two cast-iron grave covers, reminding us that we are in the industrial heartland of early modern Sussex. One has the inscription around the edge, as if it were a carved stone slab, whilst the other is very up to date with the inscription set in three ribbons across the centre. Yet they are just five years apart. Easily missed on the wall is a twentieth-century memorial brass remembering Ann Tree, one of the Protestant martyrs of Sussex who was executed at East Grinstead in July 1556. Other memorial tablets gathered up from around the church have been placed at the west end and include a charming portrait medallion of Elizabeth Wetherell who died in 1831 aged just twenty-seven.

49. WESTMESTON, ST MARTIN

Standing on a very busy bend, St Martin's Church could only be in Sussex. Its catslide roof on the south side is covered in its lower slopes with Horsham slab, whilst it's upper reaches are of red tile. The diminutive belfry is covered with wooden shingles. This is one of the things that makes Sussex churches stand out – there is a greater variety of building materials here than you find elsewhere. The inside displays the simplest form of thirteenth-century architecture, with a two-bay fourteenth-century south aisle added onto a two-cell Norman church. The whole building suffered from an over-ambitious Victorian restoration when the stonework was recut and a new roof structure installed. However, it is not the building itself that attracts visitors as much as the stained glass. The east window dates from 1873 and was made by J. B. Capronnier of Brussels. Its strident colouring is a catalogue piece, the designs in the tracery above just filling in the space rather than relating to the images below. He was popular in England in the 1850s and 1860s but by the 1870s he was being overtaken by home-grown English designers like Charles Eamer Kempe. His is the west window which depicts the legend of St Martin dividing his cloak for a beggar. Although Kempe used the same medieval Flemish designs as inspiration, his colours are more muted and the figures more lifelike. The window even contains a paragraph

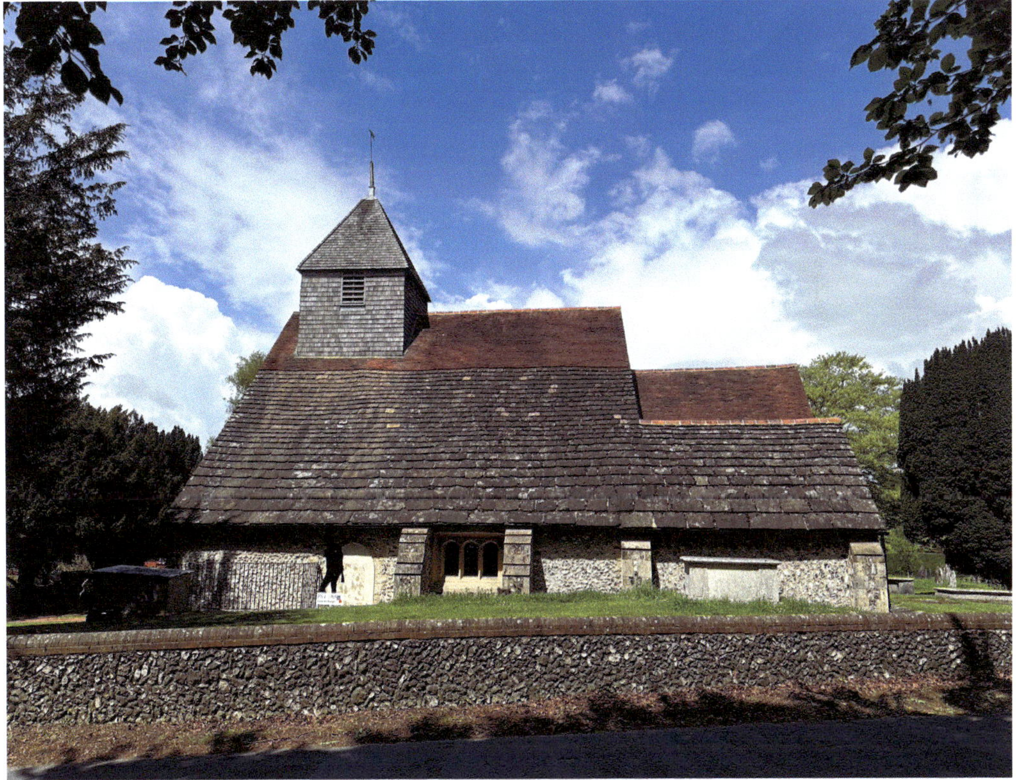

Westmeston. The huge catslide roof is mainly of Horsham slab, graduated with the largest at the bottom and smallest at the top where it gives way to much lighter clay tiles.

about St Martin for those unfamiliar with his story! Like so many Victorian firms, Kempe produced windows in such huge numbers that his studios became more like a production line, reusing designs time and again. This led to the revolution that became known as the Arts and Crafts movement where everything was a one-off, specifically produced for its location. Here at Westmeston, in the north wall of the nave is one of the best examples of an Arts and Crafts window in Sussex. It's a memorial to a local man killed in the First World War and is the work of Reginald Hallward. It depicts a dashing St George on horseback above a sleeping town, with three angels above. I would like to think that the brass inscription beneath the window with a delightful enamel shield of arms is also by Hallward.

50. WINCHELSEA, ST THOMAS A BECKET

Winchelsea is, thankfully, quieter than its near neighbour Rye where the streets teem with tourists and the church is a major attraction. Yet of the two it is Winchelsea's church that is far more important architecturally and contains some premier-rank furnishings. Its story starts in the late thirteenth century when a new town was established here, populated by merchants who had lost their original settlement to the sea at the bottom of the hill. The quality of the church shows that masons of the highest skill worked on the building, probably under the patronage of King Edward I who was closely involved with the town's establishment. Unfortunately, that patronage didn't continue for long and the church was never completed. The town was based almost exclusively on one trade – the importation of wine – and many houses retain their original undercrofts, but this trade fell into decline and coastal raids by the French didn't help. So, the church we have today is really only the chancel and its chapels. The ruined walls which dominate the exterior are of the east end of proposed transepts, and the nave would have carried on towards the western wall of today's churchyard. The interior is notable for two reasons. Firstly, for the medieval effigies which line the walls, and secondly for the twentieth-century stained glass. The monuments are set under elaborate canopies constructed in the walls and planned from the start, most likely of benefactors to the new building. Tradition ascribes most of them to the Alard family, known wine merchants. The effigies in the north aisle are carved in Purbeck marble, and those in the south are limestone. Together they form one of the best series of monuments in a Sussex church. Ten stunning stained-glass windows were designed by the Scottish artist Douglas Strachan (d. 1950) and paid for by Lord Blanesborough. The three on the north side form the village war memorial. One has a tiny scene of King Edward I looking at a plan of the church which is under construction. Next to it, and illustrative of how our interpretation of history can change, is a scene showing monks carrying the tombs now in the church up from the old church by the sea. It was long thought that this is what happened. However, we now know that the tombs date from the time when the present church was completed. In the churchyard is the grave of comedian Spike Milligan (d. 2002), with an inscription in Gaelic.

51. WITHYHAM, ST MICHAEL AND ALL ANGELS

Like many ancient churches dedicated to St Michael, this stands on a high promontory above its village. Since his visionary appearance on a hill in Italy, St Michael has always been associated with high places, a link between earth and Heaven.

The church we visit today is one of the most altered in Sussex, having been rebuilt in the mid-seventeenth century after being struck by lightning. Externally it is a jumble of rooflines with a long catslide roof on the south side complete with dormer window. The sundial over the porch tells all as it records the date 1672, which must record the culmination of rebuilding. The date 1737 also appears, which probably marks a recalibration of the dial. Inside we find a dark interior of ashlar stone and our eyes are drawn to the remains of wall paintings over the chancel arch which are nineteenth century in date. By the door is the elegant font, boldly dated 1666, and two cast-iron grave markers. If you think the interior is odd, it is because the north arcade was not rebuilt after the fire – perhaps it was too badly damaged – and a single roof was constructed which covers nave and aisle. In the north-east corner of the church is the Sackville Chapel, the goal for most visitors. It is still privately owned by the Sackville family, the senior branch of which lives here (with the more famous but junior branch living at Knole in Kent). In the centre of the chapel is one of the most moving monuments in the country – to the thirteen-year-old Thomas Sackville who died in 1677. It was carved by Caius Cibber, a young Danish sculptor who had studied in Italy and whose best-known work is the relief on the base of The Monument in London. Here he put the young man lying on a chest tomb, holding a skull with his

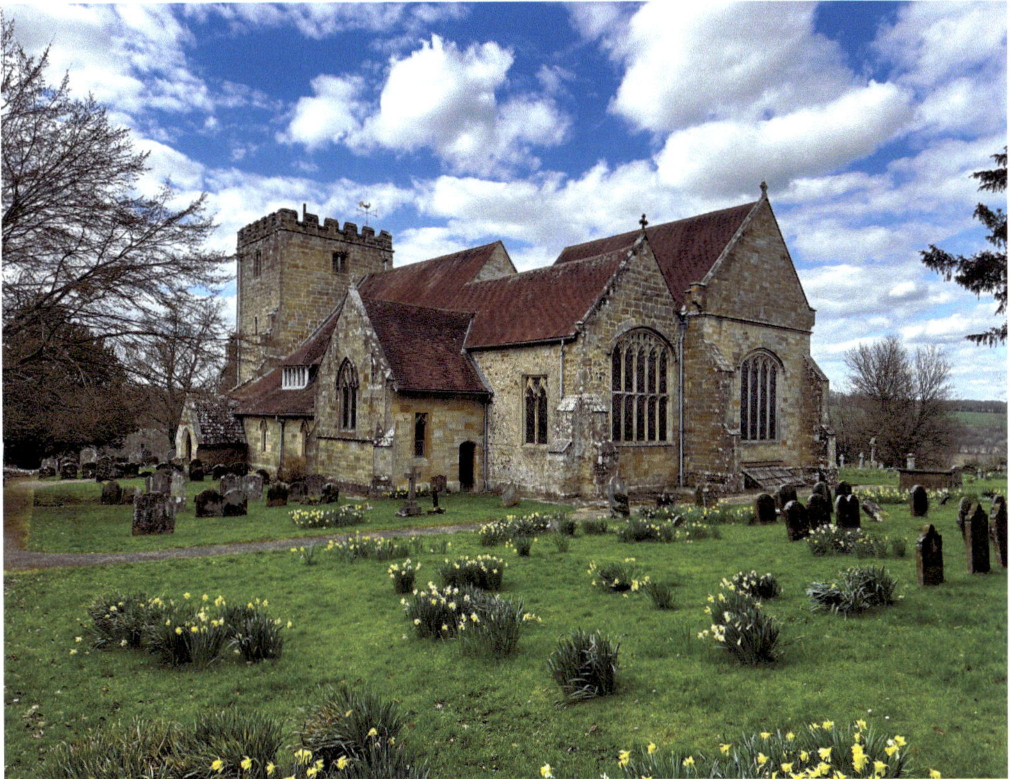

Withyham. The present church was rebuilt after a lightning strike in the seventeenth century. On the right-hand side the taller roof is that of the privately owned Sackville Chapel.

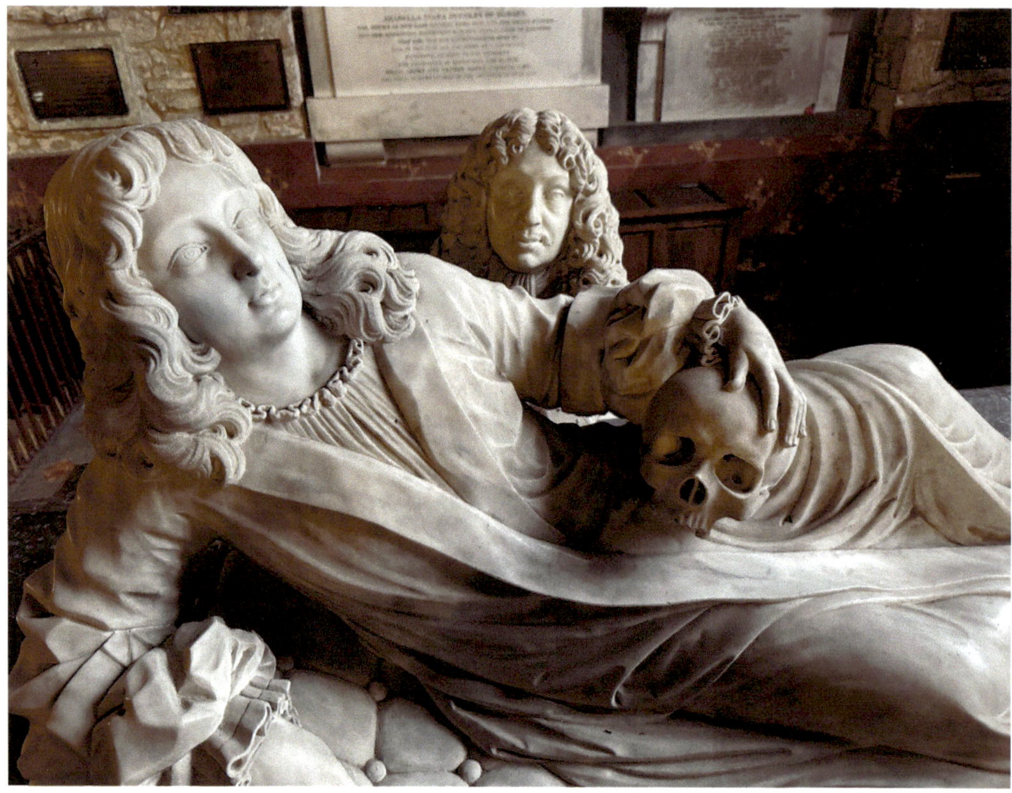

Withyham. The touching free-standing monument to thirteen-year-old Thomas Sackville who died in 1677.

parents kneeling either side. Rather than being a stiff, formal grouping, it is a lifelike composition and you can see the concern, not just in the parents' expressions, but in their poses. The chapel, contained within its original iron railing, contains memorials to many later members of the family including one to Arabella, Duchess of Dorset (d. 1825) which is signed by Sir Francis Chantrey. It shows her sorrowing daughters in a familiar composition for the period, some 150 years after Cibber had introduced the concept of naturalistic funerary carving. The vault also contains the remains of writer and gardener Vita Sackville-West who died in 1962.